SOME MEMORIES

GROWING UP WITH MARTY ROBBINS

As remembered by his twin sister Mamie and told to Andrew Means

Andrew Means

ACKNOWLEDGMENTS

Juanita Buckley and the Friends of Marty Robbins for their encouragement and encyclopedic knowledge of Marty's life and work.

Mamie's son Michael Ramsey for his support.

Table of Contents

Preface

"Some memories just won't die," country music legend Marty Robbins sang in one of his final recordings before his death from heart failure on December 8th, 1982.

Memories of his family and upbringing in Arizona were clearly very important to Marty. His music resonates with the culture and stories of the Southwestern United States, and in his songs are deeply personal reflections on the bonds of home and family.

Not surprisingly, Marty's twin sister Mamie had similar feelings about the upbringing they had shared in and around Phoenix, Arizona. After her brother suffered his fatal heart attack, she set down some of those memories on paper and tape.

In 1984 I met Mamie while I was researching a newspaper story about her brother's Arizona connections. She mentioned that their childhood in the central Arizona desert would be a good basis for a book, and that piqued my interest.

In conversations over the next few months, Mamie Robinson-Minotto — as she was then — and I reconstructed the events and impressions the two siblings had experienced as children. Mamie revealed that she and her brother had discussed compiling an account of their childhood. But the story couldn't be complete without drawing from the memories of other family members.

For earlier family history — details about their colorful cowboy grandfather, 'Texas Bob' Heckle, for instance — Mamie sometimes fell back on the recollections of her older sisters, Ann and Lillie.[1]

No one but Mamie, however, could describe their own childhood with such authority. After all, the twins were often left to their own devices. They wandered a desert with a fraction of today's population, frequently with only each other for company.

Where our writing project started to tail off was at the point where Marty began to be recognized in a major way for his singing talent. Though the twins remained close in spirit, adulthood inevitably put physical distance between them.

While Mamie stayed in or near her home state for the most part, Marty changed his last name from Robinson to Robbins, moved to Nashville and embarked on the world travels that his career demanded. The two met when they could, and still confided in each other. But Mamie could no longer claim to be an eye witness to her brother's every move.

As far as their childhood went though, Mamie's account gives a fascinating insight into a bygone era and the early development of a brother who would become internationally famous.

Despite the enthusiasm we both felt for Mamie's memoir however, publishers we approached seemed reluctant to commit. Perhaps they were too far removed from the desert to find this phase of Marty's life compelling. And so notes, tapes and nascent manuscript languished almost, but not quite, forgotten.

A collection of images, *Marty Robbins: The Photographic Journal of Marty's Family*, was published privately by Mamie in 1985, but with just a brief description of each picture. The photos had been passed down by her mother Emma, who was apparently quite a camera enthusiast. They were all that remained from a much bigger collection of pictures and memorabilia that were lost in a fire in Emma's home in the Sunnyslope district of north Phoenix in the early 1970s.

Twenty years later it still gnawed at me that the recollections I had recorded from Mamie had never been made public. Sadly, Mamie had passed away on March 14th, 2004. But there was now a museum to commemorate Marty, situated where he grew up. Surely there were country music fans and, for that matter, Arizona history buffs who would enjoy this background. Perhaps it was time to have another go.

To make the decision easier, the publishing industry had changed radically in the 20 years since Mamie and I had first contemplated this volume. New technology, boosted by computers and the Internet, made it feasible to publish and market independently on a relatively low budget. With encouragement from the Friends of Marty Robbins, the organization behind the museum, and the proviso that I'd work in my own good time with no fixed deadline, I was ready and willing to have another go at getting Mamie's memoirs into print.

The first task was to dust off those notes and tapes and familiarize myself with them again. The gist of the story was as I remembered it, of course. But there were many forgotten details and impressions. The sheer hardship of this family's day to day life, for instance, was so vividly described by Mamie.

Imagine bringing up a brood of children in tents in the desert, and walking miles to school or the store. Think of those summers with no air conditioned houses or vehicles, heat shimmering off every surface and every object hot to the touch. In today's world of malls, cell phones and TV ads, it's a stretch to contemplate a childhood in which toys were mostly what you could invent in the surrounding trees and bushes, or what could be rescued from other people's trash.

For their mother, parenthood must have seemed endless. The eldest of her nine children, Pat, was 15 years older than Martin and Mamie, and her youngest, Harley and Charley, were five years younger.

As children, as Mamie mentioned, they didn't give much thought about how their own circumstances compared to others. Their various jerrybuilt homes in the desert north of Phoenix, and eventually in the small farming town of Glendale, were measured by opportunity for play rather than social status.

Only later in life did she realize that some of their friends were no better off. In many respects then, their story reflects those of numerous unheralded Arizonans in the 1920s and '30s. The difference of course was that one of the Robinsons escaped deprivation to go on to fame and fortune.

Understandably, their family circumstances were not something they wanted to boast about as young adults.

"There was a point in my life where I was very much ashamed of the Robinsons and Heckles," admitted Mamie, adding that her brother felt much the same way. "It was not because of being poor but (because) of appearing to like being poor. It was the attitude."

As the twins entered their teenage years their interests began to diverge and they spent less time together. Marty's activities and opinions from this period were not so vivid in her memory.

When Marty was interviewed about his early years, after he had become a star, his account didn't always fit with Mamie's. There were some episodes, such as Marty's frequent expeditions to Glendale to see movies, to say nothing of his declared exploits as a railriding hobo and bronco buster, about which Mamie had little or nothing to say.

Apparently she didn't share her brother's enthusiasm for cowboy movies and his particular devotion to the singing cowboy Gene Autry. Leastwise she appears not to have accompanied him on his long walks from home to watch movies in Glendale.

She knew enough about these trips, however, to contradict the accepted version of this story — that Marty picked cotton to earn the admission money. Could it be that, in later years, Marty just wanted to embellish his bio with a little more color? Or perhaps there were just some things that Marty kept from his sister.

Whether he kept his musical ambitions to himself is another consideration. Around the time of our conversations, Mamie told interviewer Sandy Lovejoy of Phoenix country music station, KNIX, that as kids "Marty didn't dream of being a singer." They used to whistle and sing together on their jaunts into the desert, but there was no discussion about singing being a goal in life. Maybe, as for many other boys and young men, the promising combination of girls, guitars and glamour swayed the potential troubadour.[2]

From what I can recall, Mamie also glossed over the more troubled aspects of young Marty's life. Understandably, she wouldn't have been keen to dwell on him dropping out of high school and stories about him becoming something of a local mischief maker. Columbia Records' biography of Marty refers to "minor brushes with the law," without going into detail.

Even Marty was quoted as saying he was "pretty wild" and "really wasn't a good student" when he attended grade school in Peoria and Glendale High School.[3]

From that time on, Marty's life story began to drift more and more beyond her vision. He went on to join the Navy, returning to Glendale to work at a series of menial jobs before finding his musical vocation. Mamie, meanwhile, was pursuing her own course as a wife and mother.

Fortunately, there were others still around who knew Marty from this period. For instance, there was the late Frankie Starr, who proudly recounted his encounters with Marty when they were both performing in local clubs. Being a little older than the future celebrity, Frankie regarded himself as something of a mentor to Marty. Mamie and I also interviewed a Navy buddy who remembered a couple of Marty's pranks from their days in the service.

Over the years since Marty's death, others who knew him from youth have been interviewed by local newspapers and fan newsletters. There's no doubt that much could have been added to the material in this book. Former neighbors and school friends have recounted their own anecdotes about Marty and his exploits as a youngster.

In addition, his marriage to a Glendale girl, Marizona, birth of their children Ronnie and Janet, and the career that took him from local clubs and radio to Nashville could spawn many chapters in their own right.

It seems appropriate to me, however, to keep the focus for this volume on Mamie's memories of their childhood. During those formative years the twins were virtually inseparable and Mamie had little competition for her brother's attention. These, I feel sure, were among the most treasured tokens for both Marty and Mamie.

To any reader who is confused by the changes in point of view in the narrative, I can only offer an apology. Sometimes the text is written as if it's coming direct from Mamie and sometimes it refers to her in the third person. Even if Mamie and I had completed this book together, I think we would have faced this problem. There were parts of the family history, Marty's naval service and relationship with Frankie Starr that inevitably drew on sources other than Mamie. By incorporating these other voices, I can only hope that the continuity of the story is not disrupted — or, if it is, that the additional material makes the extra effort on the part of the reader worthwhile.

I've done my best to be true to what I think Mamie's concept of this account would have been. Undoubtedly we would have expanded it if we had completed the task together, and no doubt too she would have been invaluable in pointing out inaccuracies.

Marty left such a legacy that anecdotes and references relating to his story are almost inexhaustible. The man had many sides to his life and talent, and left many memories. As for the child, no one is better qualified to tell the story than his twin sister.

Notes
[1] Lillie wrote her own account of childhood, which, at the time of this writing, could be found on the Internet at http://www.geocities.com/helenshields/PAGES/gailg.html?20051. Being a little older than Mamie, Lillie has a better memory of the details of the family's several homes — the earlier ones at least. There are also some interesting parallels, such as both girls idolizing a brother. For Mamie, it was Martin. For Lillie, it was the eldest, Pat, fictionalized in her account as "Matt."

[2] KNIX publication *Tune-In*, September 1988

[3] *Phoenix Gazette*, December 9th, 1982

According to Jess Nicks, a boyhood friend of Marty (and not the same man who fathered Fleetwood Mac singer and longtime Phoenix homeowner Stevie Nicks), Marty worked at a swamp cooler repair shop after dropping out of school, "strumming his guitar when business was slow." *The Glendale Star*, September 11th, 1992. Others remember him having guitar lessons and taking part in local talent contests. So clearly he was performing as a singer, accompanying himself on guitar, before joining the Navy in 1943.

It was during this period of odd jobs, so we're told, that he wrote his first song, "Heartsick." *Hillbilly & Cowboy Hitparade*, Fall 1953.

Introduction

Martin Robinson, as he then was, and Mamie were born in a two-room house near the farm town of Glendale, a few miles northwest of Phoenix. They were born five minutes apart on September 26th 1925, with Marty appearing first at 9:55 pm.

Unlike many settlements in central Arizona, and certainly unlike the frontier towns Marty wrote about in his songs, Glendale was founded as a peaceful farming town. Among its first residents were German and Russian members of pacifist religious sects, and its initial ordinances included prohibition of alcohol.

Irrigation enabled this desert community to thrive when William J. Murphy and other pioneers channeled water through their newly dug Arizona Canal in the mid 1880s. A cosmopolitan population of Japanese, Chinese, Basques and others followed, although there were still less than 3,000 residents when Martin and Mamie were born.

Supposedly the town received its name from Polish settlers who came from Glendale, Pennsylvania. If so, it would be an appropriate connection to the Robinsons' own Polish forebears.

The entire area has changed dramatically since Mamie and Marty were kids, and the sites of their early homes in Cactus and Glendale have long since been absorbed by suburbs and busy roads. The creosote bushes, palo verde and mesquite trees that must have been the backdrop to the twins' activities have been replaced by neatly clipped landscaping. Many of the desert creatures have gone, along with the hogs, chickens, dairy cows and vegetable gardens that seemed so commonplace back then. Only the school they attended in Peoria, now a city museum, gives much sense of what their lives were like.

In any case, the twins were rarely given much opportunity to get attached to their surroundings in these early years. Like homes before and homes to come, their birthplace would not remain the family residence long. Headed by a father frequently battling the bottle and the law, this was a family of drifters. Even the original family name of Maczinski was changed, apparently in an effort to escape legalities.

Martin, we're told, had the makings of an entertainer from an early age. Performing just seemed to be in his blood, whether it was singing in church or playing a role in the school play. No doubt it didn't hurt that he could do no wrong in his mother's eyes and, despite their differences, even his father seems to have gone along much of the time with Martin's natural aptitude for the spotlight.

Friction between father and the rest of the family must have been a continual source of stress. Mamie recalled Martin said how much he hated his father. But she knew he didn't mean it. They had too much fun together, she explained.

Perhaps this childhood exposure to the ups and downs of adult temperament instilled resilience in Martin. Another characteristic that recurs through Mamie's account is Martin's ability to shrug off setbacks.

Whether it was a spanking from a teacher or roughhousing with his older brothers, Martin seems to have had the fortitude and courage to deal with physical pain and mental pressure that might have upset others. Leastwise, he didn't let it show when he was hurt. It was a quality, one can imagine, that would stand him in good stead years later when he took up NASCAR racing.

Appropriately, Marty was known for the loyalty of his fans. He was never one to put himself above or apart from others, and people responded to that down-to-earth sincerity. At the same time, he valued his privacy. He was known to sneak back unannounced to the desert where he grew up, for instance occasionally staying at Apache Junction's Superstition Inn (later renamed the Grand Hotel). Mamie was in no doubt that if he couldn't have afforded to fly back when he had the time, he wouldn't have continued to live in Nashville.

"He loved Arizona," Mamie said. " ... I know there were many times he would have traded everything he had just to go back to this time of his life when he had no worries, no burdens."[1]

As was the case for so many young men of his generation, Marty had to complete his military service in World War Two before devoting himself to a career. He returned to Glendale in 1947 after discharge from the Navy, and soon became a fixture in local clubs.

Reportedly he shortened his last name to Robbins to protect his family's privacy, although Mamie said he wasn't happy with his stage name at first and wished he hadn't adopted it.

Mamie, incidentally, dismissed another anecdote from those times — that at first Marty performed with the name Jack Robinson. Still, she didn't have an answer for why the family used the name Robinson in the first place. Why Marty's father chose that particular alias is a mystery. Now there's something to think about. The singer of "El Paso" and all those other hits might have become known to us under a different name entirely.

N otes

[1] KNIX publication *Tune-In*, September 1988.

Chapter One
Growing Up in the Desert
— As Remembered by Mamie

From today's point of view, when children have so many toys and forms of entertainment available to them, the desert must seem a very Spartan playground. But for us it was full of interesting things to do anddiscover.

The memories are vivid and precious, and without doubt the inspiration for many of Marty's ballads.

We had many questions, like most kids, but could find no one with the time for answers. So we came up with our own, which boiled down to one thing: God made everything that was good and the Devil made everything that was bad. It was simple, but it satisfied us at the time.

Although raised in poverty and at times domestic violence, and with no visible guidelines to speak of much of the time, we still got a good dose of old time religion — with its accompanying feelings of guilt.

"God's going to get you for that" or "You're going to Hell" were the admonishments for doing something bad, and it all depended on who thought they had been wronged. Religion, discipline — nothing was consistent, except poverty. But we were taught never to question adults, and so we didn't.

The desert, however, gave us a refuge from the harsh concerns of the adult world. A small clump of bushes or low mesquite trees could become a house with many rooms, a store, a school, or whatever our imaginations decided upon. We would sing, or pretend we were in school — even before we were old enough for school. Mostly we roamed and explored. Every day there was something new to us.

When it rained real hard on the desert at certain times of year, it would bring out tiny frogs that had been hibernating in the ground. There would be millions of them, and we thought it had rained frogs. We had lots of fun putting these little critters in jars and matchboxes, and wondering if they lived by Jesus up in the sky. We were thoroughly convinced that was where they came from and no one could tell us any different.

We wandered the fresh, clean desert after the rains in complete happiness. There is nothing to compare to the scent of the creosote bush after the rain has washed the dust from its leaves.

When the rains had gone and our little frogs had gone back to the sky, the ground became very dry and hard, parched and checkered like old pieces of pottery. We then had another challenge to our imagination. The pieces of earth were easy to pick up and we stacked them like adobes to make houses.

Sometimes, for a change, we would build a fort and pretend that we were fighting off Indians. Our adobe walls were fragile though, and didn't last long before crumbling back to dirt. They were not as pretty as sand castles on the beach perhaps, but we were just as proud of our handiwork.

We were making use of the materials available to us, just as we're bidden by the old saying about doing as the Romans do when in Rome.

Besides, no one ever loved the beach any better than we loved the desert at any time of the year. Of course, the summers were the best, with more hours of daylight and no cold.

It was a love that Martin had all his life. He told me many times that when he was close, or getting close, to the desert and Arizona, he would get the urge to write. Except for the urge to write, I feel the same way.

All of our running, roaming and dreaming gave us good appetites. So when supper was ready we did not have to be called twice.

We had good food when things were going relatively well. Fresh vegetables, fresh butter and milk, plus Mom could make the best yeast rolls. All this made a feast for which we were truly grateful.

When Dad was in a good mood, we could talk him into entertaining us on the harmonica and dance his happy Polish jigs. Maybe the next day he would be in a bad mood. But for that night he was fun to be around, and I could forget the fear of him that consumed me most of the time. Martin never seemed to be afraid of him, and — when he was old enough — would join him in the dances and take turns with him on the harmonica.

Martin was always making some kind of music. When he was about four he was already playing a Jew's harp as well as mouth organ. Just sitting at the table he'd take a knife or fork and hit on everything and try different sounds.

My sister Lillie tells a story about hearing church music, or rather what she thought was church music, coming from somewhere in the house. She knew the phonograph was not playing, and we didn't have a radio at the time. Eventually she tracked the sounds down. It was Martin in his bed, his head covered by his sheet and blanket, playing the harmonica.

Often we would gather around the big cast-iron wood stove that provided heat for the house as well as for cooking. Summers were not a problem. But I remember bone-chilling cold in the winter, unless we were running or standing huddled around that old stove. In the morning we didn't need any nagging to get us to dress in a hurry.

Fortunately wood was plentiful, and in winter there was a fire going constantly. When we came in from our chores, from school or play, there would often be a pot of rabbit stew cooking away or a big stewing hen. The old house would smell good. But whatever the menu, we ate with 'mucho gusto.'

The fear returned for all of us on those nights Dad didn't come in from his route when he was due. None of us slept well, if at all, until he came in and we knew whether he was 'good' drunk or mean drunk.

The picture of my mother keeping a vigil at the window until she could see his headlights in the distance will remain with me as long as I live. She had time then to quickly get in bed, and we would all pretend to be asleep.

We had kept the fire stoked so the house would not get cold, because we knew that a cold house would set off a fit of anger in him. Immediately he would make the boys get out of bed to build up the fire. If he was real angry, he would make Mom go out and chop wood — even though there was plenty already cut.

A terrible man? Yes, I suppose he was. There aren't any excuses I can make for him and these actions, except to try and remember the few moments of joy that he did provide. We have no way of knowing what private sorrows drove him to behave this way. As children, we certainly were not privy to our father's inner thoughts.

Early letters to my mother from him showed a very caring and loving side to his nature. The fact remains too that he did not abandon his large family — although it would have been the kindest thing he could have done.

Looking back, it is hard to believe that my mother put up with so much from him. She was a strong person. But, in her defense, she was also a victim of her own upbringing.

She was raised in remote mountain country, much the way she raised her own brood. The male in the family was always right and it was her place to stand by him, though I am sure she must have known he was wrong so much of the time. It didn't mean that she never wanted any better or that she didn't love her children. It was just that this was the life women expected in those days. She did the best she could under the worst of circumstances.

Regardless of our dad's unpredictable behavior, he was the one responsible for first pointing Martin in a musical direction. I'm sure, however, that he was never aware of it. The talent was there from the start and Martin was never discouraged from using it. To be accurate, it must be added that he was never openly encouraged either.

Chapter Two
Favorite Child

Martin was Mom's favorite child and there was never any doubt of that. The feeling was mutual, and he never lost that love or ever stopped wanting to do as much as he could for her. I never remember a time when she got mad at him, criticized or abused him in any way, verbally or physically. She must have known he was special in some way.

Her support might even have been what made him special — or at least have the drive that he had to go forward without fear. He may have been self-conscious and awkward in his early years, but never afraid. Mom was very generous with him, with what little she had, and eventually he was able to repay her.

I believe some of his songs were written with her in mind.

She did spoil him and make him a bit obnoxious to others at times, but she seemed unaware of it. He was her only topic of conversation, even before he became a success. It seemed to me that he was always allowed to do exactly what he wanted to do. Looking back years later, I used to say that if he had robbed a bank mother would have said the bank shouldn't have been there.

Even at an early age, Martin seemed enterprising and independent. When we were five, he decided one time he was going to run away from home. He had got mad at my mother.

To me, she didn't seem nearly concerned enough about Martin's threat to run away. She just said: "Go on. You'll be home for supper."

I started crying, and pleaded: "Don't run away from home."

But he left anyway, and I thought Mom was so cruel to let him go.

"How can you let him go?" I demanded.

But she just stayed calm and, as Martin was walking out of the house, she asked;

"Here, do you want to take some clothes with you?"

Martin shook his head and just kept walking.

Now that I look back on it, I realize he couldn't have gone any further than the fence. But I thought at the time he was gone for ever, and I was screaming and crying.

"Look what you've done," I told Mother. "You're so cruel."

I was the one who got the spanking, because I wouldn't shut up. Pretty soon Martin was back. I was so glad to see him. Mom could see him all the time. She knew where he was. But I was scared to death.

If there was any mischief to be done, it seemed as if Martin would be there.

We had a basement in the house where Mom stored homemade root beer, mostly to keep it out of sight and out of our hands. She managed very well with all of us but Martin.

I'm sure she thought she had him under control, until one day she decided to treat us all to a cool drink. When she went downstairs to get our treat, she found a nail hole in the top of each of the bottles. Her 'little angel' had come up with this method of stealing a sly drink because he couldn't find where Mom had hidden the bottle opener.

As I recall, I think he did get into a little trouble with Mom on that occasion. I am sure, however, that he had to stay out of reach of the rest of us — particularly his older brothers — for some time. I was mad because he dared to do this terrible thing without me. Mom's next step, I expect, was to hide the hammer and nails, although I don't remember him doing that particular trick ever again.

Whenever we were given candy Martin would try out another favorite ploy. He would always eat his faster than I would, and then take mine. Finally, in self defense, I decided on a plan to stop this. As soon as we received candy, I would lick every part of it right in front of him. For some reason, he didn't want it after that.

Given half the chance, I would join in Martin's little adventures — or at least, offer encouragement from the sideline.

I was the only one who thought it was funny, for instance, when he would climb up into our drinking water tank for a cooling swim.

Our other companion in mischief was our big black-and-white part-collie dog, named Whitey. He was always with us. That is until we wanted to pretend he was a horse and try and ride him or tie him up to a wagon and make him pull us. He, like me, knew when to find a nice thick bush or some other place to hide. Our dogs all seemed to know the same trick.

I liked to lie down with our warm, furry dog, suck my thumb, twist my hair and go to sleep. The boys would wait until I was asleep and then call to the dog. He would jump up and I would go flying, and of course start crying. Martin would come over and try to console me. I know he was really sorry — but it never stopped him from doing it.

The dogs were not the only animals to provide us with some amusement. We loved the pigs too, and played a lot around the pens. The old sow named Florence — we gave them all names — was real mean, and would attack anyone who came near her pen. Of course Martin would tease her until she would almost jump out of her pen, and then he would run away. I would be petrified as usual.

Sometimes the animals got their own back on Martin. Once, the older boys tied a small wagon to a horse and put Martin in it. The horse bolted, throwing Martin 'ass over appetite.' I went running and screaming to him, to find him brushing himself off and laughing like a crazy person. The boys were disappointed that he wasn't hurt and wanted to try the stunt again. But he had had enough. He must have been hurt, although he never let anyone know it. Perhaps, once out of sight, he whimpered a little.

Did Martin have more than his share of self-confidence? I don't think so. But he did have a lot of guts. He never hung back. He didn't mind making a fool of himself. I know he was never secure, however, no matter what his accomplishments were. This is why he was so private as an adult.

I do remember one occasion when he was visibly shaken up. In fact we both were.

Dad was going to teach Mom how to drive the car. I suppose he thought it would be safe enough to let her have the wheel out in the middle of nowhere. On the other hand, maybe his judgment had been affected by one of his alcoholic blackouts. Why a man with no patience, a violent temper, and probably a severe hangover would even undertake this project remains a mystery.

Anyway, Martin and I jumped in the back of the truck all ready for this 'fun experience.' It was a fiasco from the first change of gear, and quickly ceased to be a fun trip for the two of us in the back. Our giggles turned to stark terror. Fear does not describe it. For us two kids it was indeed terrifying.

It seemed like twenty hands were grabbing for the gearshift and steering wheel, and as many feet reaching for the brakes. Dad did everything but jump out and put rocks in front of the wheels to stop that old truck.

Off the old road we went and into a bed of sand at what seemed like break neck speed, but may have been only twenty five miles per hour. Dad was cursing and Mom crying. Martin and I panicked and jumped overboard. The sand provided a smooth landing as we rolled over in the wake of the runaway truck. If we hadn't been so scared it might even have been fun.

We lay there and speechlessly watched the truck come to a stop. The only noise was Dad's violent swearing and pitiful crying from Mom. We looked at each other and began to laugh like crazy with relief.

Needless to say, we walked home. Even when Mom and Dad were almost out of sight, we could hear them yelling at each other over the noise of the old Model-T. Later, we would think about it and laugh with each other. But we never dared mention it to them.

Every family has its little hell raiser and rebel, but I'm positive there was none more charming than ours. A smile and a funny face brought forgiveness every time as far as my mother and I were concerned.

Of course charm, like beauty, is in the eye of the beholder and I'm sure his brothers didn't see this quality in him. Why else would they chase him into the brush and the desert, just because he did one little thing like throw a rock at them from behind the outhouse — or worse still, while they were in it?

Martin could throw straight — as well as run straight, and fast! This he frequently had to do in self-defense. He made an elusive target as he disappeared into thickets of mesquite and palo verde, and was seldom hit by the barrage of stones and sticks thrown at him by his older brothers, Johnny and Red. He would stay hidden until he thought they had forgotten about him.

When he was hit, he never cried. He just fought back like a tiger. He sometimes cried make-believe tears, but only if he thought it would get his brothers into trouble for hurting him. Often this trick worked, and for a time at least it would stop the open warfare. The pinching and punching had to continue out of sight.

I always wanted to get in and help him, and sometimes did. But being a coward, and establishing that fact early on, I usually reverted to running back in and 'telling' on our brothers. I must have saved Martin many lumps that way.

Chapter Three
Family Roots

Although Martin's childhood in the desert around Phoenix is the focus of Mamie's account, there should be a place in it for some family history. After all, the family — particularly on their mother's side — had strong connections to Arizona.

Martin's grandfather on the maternal side was 'Texas Bob' Heckle, a surname the family believed to be of German derivation. He was a genuine Western character, so we're told, who produced a brood of cattle-herding sons and became something of a minor legend in his own right.

"Snowy white hair to his shoulders, bronzed and wiry, he was the picture of a frontiersman" in his prime. As chronicled by Mamie, his career included "Confederate soldier in his teens, an Indian scout for General George Crook and later owned and operated freight wagons while he homesteaded and ranched in the early territorial days of Arizona."[1]

Among other accomplishments, 'Texas Bob' was a poet and storyteller, and it seems that some of his anecdotes influenced Martin's songwriting. He, or his kin at any rate, is even mentioned in connection with one of the West's classic cowboy songs, "The Sierry Petes" (also known as "Tying Knots In The Devil's Tail"), by the late versifier, Gail Gardner, of Prescott, Arizona.[2]

Not much was passed down about their grandmother on that side of the family, as far as Mamie was aware. Anna Carpenter Heckle was said to be part Indian and a Utah-born Mormon. A picture of grandmother confirmed that she did "look Indian," Mamie said. "She has those high cheek bones." In that regard Polish and Indian look something alike, Mamie added, referring to both sides of the Robinson heritage.

At any rate, Anna married Texas Bob on her 14th birthday over the objections of her mother, Emma Smith Carpenter of Annabella, Utah. They had 13 children, and lived in Texas and New Mexico besides Arizona.

In a frontier family such as theirs at the turn of the 20th century, everyone had to share in a daily routine of farming and ranching chores. Not only the seven boys but the girls too learned to ride and rope. It was a work ethic that in turn would be passed down to Martin and Mamie and the rest of the Robinson brood.

Mamie gave little indication of how much time they spent with their grandfather. He appears in the story once in a while when the family needed help with a move, but Mamie didn't say how either her parents or their children got on with him. Even as adults, Mamie said, neither she nor her twin brother cared much about the family's origins for a long time.

"Then in about 1970 I sent Marty a picture of Grandad Heckle," she related. "We had seen that picture all our lives but it wasn't until Hattie, our cousin, sent me a copy that we really paid much attention.

"It looked so much like Marty it was uncanny. I had never noticed the resemblance until then. I sent it to him and said, 'Look at this,' and he agreed. After that Marty began to get more interested in him, partly because of the resemblance and it also fitted right in with the Western ballads."[3]

In his later years, Texas Bob apparently became quite a well-known figure on the benches of Glendale city parks. Mamie remembered hearing as an adult from locals who used to listen to Texas Bob's stories of fighting Indians when Arizona was still the frontier.

Unfortunately, old age was not kind to him. He died in a state mental hospital, Mamie related.

"He was just senile," she said, "but in those days they didn't have anywhere else to put people. He was probably 80 or so. He was old and tottering. The beard and hair that are so pretty in his picture, I remember as ugly and very dirty."

Martin and Mamie's mother, Emma Heckle, was born June 26th 1889 in New Mexico, and raised in Arizona alongside seven brothers and five sisters. The family migrated from ranch to ranch, no doubt going where the work was. For a time they lived in the small settlement of Oracle, north east of Tucson.[4]

Long before Marty and Mamie were born, Emma was mother to two children in a previous marriage.

As Mamie recounted from family history — probably as she heard it from her older sisters — Emma married her first husband on May 25th, 1909.[5]

Mamie continued the sequence of events as follows:

His name was Dan C. Cavaness and he came from a prominent northern Arizona ranching family. The reason for these nuptials between a couple of such different backgrounds is not hard to guess.

"Apparently even in those days they got pregnant before they got married," Mamie commented. "So the old man (Heckle) took a shotgun and said, 'Marry my daughter.'"

The marriage was frowned on by the Cavaness family, however, and the couple didn't stay together long.

"I remember my mother saying they worked really hard to break it up," Mamie said.

It was long enough though to set up home and produce two children, Robert Mathew "Pat" and Anna Mae. They lived first on a sheep and goat ranch in the Bradshaw Mountains, south of Prescott, where Pat was born in 1910. They then moved to Gillett, a former stage stop on the road down towards Phoenix, where Ann was born, and finally they followed a job lead to Mesa.

Seven months after Ann was born, the father left and went back to his ancestral ranch near Flagstaff. After the divorce Emma took care of the children alone. She cleaned houses and did laundry and anything she could do to keep the kids with her.

She was living in an area on the east side of Phoenix, in what is now Scottsdale.[6] Mail reached her via the Scottsdale Stage. Later there was a brief marriage to a man named Hicks. He was seldom mentioned in subsequent years, and if his name was brought up she had nothing to say. So he remains a mystery.

Our parents met after she moved farther into Phoenix. She was working in a boarding house on East Washington Street when she met the man who fathered her next seven children.

From old letters I have found I get the impression that he lived at the boarding house. However, my sister Lillie tells me that our mother's sisters had dared her to put an ad in the paper for a husband, and he answered. I personally find this hard to believe, and since we have no evidence of either and I can't imagine my mother doing such a thing, I prefer my version.

In a letter from Mom to her father, Texas Bob, telling him of her intentions, she says: "I don't think I am making a mistake this time, Father. He is a real nice boy, that's for sure."

And there was also one from Dad to Texas Bob asking for her hand in marriage. It was very formal and sincere, with all of the plans that a man in love would make. They sounded mutually in love, and I believe they were. He was charming, young and handsome. They were married May 12th, 1917, three months after they met.

The "nice boy" had neglected to mention one small detail, which may or may not have made a difference. His name was not John J. Robinson, as she thought. That was an alias he had taken in Michigan.when he left there to avoid the draft. I've never known when she found out she had married a draft dodger of Polish descent, but I'm sure that by the time she did it didn't make any difference.

She was fiercely loyal and faithful to him throughout their marriage. She followed him wherever and whenever he wanted to go. The years that followed would take her across several states and involve various modes of travel.

Had she known what lay ahead in her marriage, I wonder if she would have made the first leg of the journey before she bailed out. On reconsidering, I don't think she would have done that. "The man is the boss" was too deeply ingrained in the women of that time, and they never thought to question it.

He first moved her and the children to Michigan, where his family lived.[7] There he was John J. Maczinski again. By this time, besides Pat and Ann, they had a baby of their own — a girl name Lillian, shortened to Lillie, who had been born in Phoenix in 1918.

Whether Robinson or Maczinski, Emma's new husband began the journey east in what would become an all too familiar way. The family left in a topless Model T he stole off a Phoenix street. In New Mexico he sold the car and bought rail tickets for the rest of the journey to Michigan.[8]

There they lived on a farm at first, and then moved to town where other family members were living.

In their letters back to Arizona they sounded happy. Dad related the trip in a letter to Texas Bob.

"Dear Father," it began, "it was one hell of a trip, but a fun trip too. The old Ford worked pretty dam hard but good too. Now we are here and every thing is just lovely."

He goes on to say he had left Mother and the babies in Lansing with family, and he was working in Detroit making 40 cents an hour and 60 cents for overtime. Within two weeks he could afford to bring them to where he was.

Mother's letters to the family in the West were full of love. She couldn't hide her homesickness from them, but did a good job of keeping it from her husband. They are sad letters, telling of cold and loneliness but still full of hope that things would turn out all right if they worked together.

Another child was born in May 1920. This time it was another boy, who in time could keep Pat company. His name was officially Johnny Raymond Maczinski, a fact that would cause him problems proving his identity to school officials and such when the Robinsons eventually returned to Arizona. As a young child, he was not aware of the name difference of course, and no one told him about it I guess.[9]

Notes

[1] *Marty Robbins: The Photographic Journal of Marty's Family.* Texas Bob joined a regiment listed as the First Texas at the age of 14, Mamie told me, and he was also said to have been a Texas Ranger and to have campaigned with Generals Custer and Crook in Montana and Wyoming.

[2] In her book *Ten Thousand Goddam Cattle - A history of the American cowboy in song, story and verse* (Katydid Books and Records, 1976), Katie Lee describes a visit with Gail Gardner in which he reminisced about working cattle — not to mention Prescott's Whiskey Row — with one Bob Heckle. Apparently this was Texas Bob's son, and thus an uncle of the Robinson brood. The younger Bob features in Gardner's song as Sandy Bob. The song credits him with helping to rope the devil. Accomplishment against great odds evidently ran in the family.

[3] Mamie's account seems to fly in the face of Marty's own reminiscences about spending hours sitting at the feet of his grandfather listening to songs and tall tales of the Old West. Indeed, Marty said "Big Iron," one of his best known gunfighter ballads, was among several sets of lyrics he based on Heckle's stories. Once again, could it be that Mamie just didn't pay so much attention to things that were of more interest to a boy?

Mamie, incidentally, had her own anecdote about 'Big Iron.' At the time Marty was composing the song, Mamie was living in the small town of Parker, just on the Arizona side of the Colorado River. Inspired no doubt by the Heckles' stomping ground on the Agua Fria river, Marty set the story in a mythical town of the same name. But he really wanted to set it in Parker, he told Mamie. Somehow there wouldn't be the same ring to lyrics that began: "To the town of Parker rode a stranger one fine day..."

[4] Family stories mention a Christmas Mine in the Oracle area, with the implication that Texas Bob was an employee there for a while. There is a Christmas Mine some 40 miles or so north east of Oracle, on state highway 77 between Winkelman and Globe. Perhaps the family moved there from Oracle. It certainly would be a long commute from Oracle back then!

[5] Yavapai County records show the marriage took place at Richinbar, the site of a mine on the east side of Interstate 17 near Bumblebee. The groom was two and a half years younger than Emma. At the time of the 1910 Federal Census, the young couple was living with his parents in a Yavapai County mining district identified as "Black Rock and Bluedam." A decade earlier, incidentally, young Dan was living near another mining town, Globe. Possibly the "prominent ranching family" Emma supposedly married into was more a reflection of the Heckles' wishful thinking.

[6] As is often the case with the family's early history, it's difficult to reconcile different versions of moves, locations and dates. In a letter to Mamie, her sister Ann wrote that after the divorce Emma and the two kids shared an address with a grocery store at 24th Street and Van Buren in Phoenix — in other words, several miles from Scottsdale. Presumably they had a room or apartment there.

[7] Elsewhere in family notes there is a mention of Manistee. Apparently this was the Maczinskis' hometown.

[8] According to Ann's letter, the car was sold in Hot Springs, New Mexico. Although there are several hot springs in that state, I was unable to decide on an obvious candidate for this location. Ann wrote that the family returned to Arizona via Hot Springs a couple of years later, so the name, or at least part of it, was firmly placed in her memory.

Ann related that they did the stretch from Hot Springs back to Arizona with a team of burros and a wagon. I'm no expert, but I would guess mules were more likely.

[9] Mamie said that she never did get along with Johnny, but that Marty adored him. Johnny was mechanically minded, and Marty took him to Nashville to work on his cars. According to *The Arizona Republic*, he died in tragic circumstances in 1966 when he was fatally injured by a concrete pipe he was unloading from a truck in the West Valley.

Chapter Four
Michigan Drifters & Arizona Cowboys

Mom became more and more homesick for the desert and her family. Her brothers and sisters were scattered over the state of Arizona. Probably for this reason, they were prolific letter writers. A visit would have meant long grueling rides by wagon or unreliable automobiles over the worst possible roads and trails.

The Heckle men were all cowboys or cow punchers and highly respected for their skill in handling cattle. They never lacked a job, because when they weren't working their own cattle they were sought after by the other ranchers. None ever became wealthy or owned any big spread of their own, but they were doing what they wanted to do.

Only one decided the range was not for him. He became civilized and married — though not necessarily in that order — and moved to California, becoming a carpenter and later a building contractor.

The open spaces of the West were what Mom was longing for and after a while, I can tell by his letters, Dad was missing them too.

Around Christmas 1920, Dad took his family by train as far as Trinidad, Colorado. They lived there until school was out. Then, in a Model T touring car with no top, they continued their journey back to Arizona. I would assume their travel was confined mostly to the daytime, because the car only had a lantern hanging on the radiator for light.

In Hot Springs, New Mexico, Dad sold the Model T and bought a team of burros and a spring wagon. I don't know exactly what a spring wagon is, but that's the story that was handed down. So that's how they continued their journey.

To feed the family and burros they would stop at farms or ranches where Dad could work and make enough money to go on until they were in need again.

Just before Christmas 1922, two years almost to the day from their departure from Michigan, they reached the Cave Creek Dam area north of Phoenix, where Mom's sister Hattie and brother-in-law were homesteading.

Grandfather Texas Bob drove a six-horse team and freight wagon out of the Gillett area, south of Black Canyon City and west of what is now Interstate 17. He and the youngest of his sons, Clarence, drove for three days to the Cave Creek area to pick up the two oldest children, Pat and Annie, and take them back to their ranch at Gillett.

Gillett was a stage coach station located to the east of the Bradshaw Mountains on the bank of the often-dry Agua Fria River.[1] The ranch was nearby. Uncle Mart and Aunt Ellen lived about ten miles down river. Shortly afterwards Granddad went back for the rest of the family left in Cave Creek. By Christmas Day everyone was together. Six uncles, four aunts, parents and grandparents. It was Heaven to the family that had been homeless for two years.

Predictably, this situation could only last a few months though. Dad was by no means a cowboy or rancher and not reclusive enough to be so isolated. That and the two overpowering personalities of Dad and Granddad must have made the living arrangements less than pleasant. So another move was on the cards.

The family went back to the Cave Creek area, and stayed with Aunt Hattie and Uncle George for about a year. They all worked to clear the land, about 120 acres, of greasewood brush and cactus. The children did not go to school during this time but were paid a tame rabbit apiece for their labor — adding more mouths to feed!

Schools were not always near. In fact there was nothing within 30 miles, and no buses, so the easiest course at the time was just not to go to school.

By the time the land was cleared the family's welcome had been worn out. They were the poor side of the family, the ones with no homestead, no money, only a lot of hungry little kids. I would imagine that, when they were seen coming, the prospect of having to provide for them sent a shiver down the spines of whichever relatives lived at the end of the road.

This must have been humiliating to my mother, who had the pride of a generation that, even though they grew up in the hills, took care of their own. Dad, being an Easterner with a totally different background — and I think of a larcenous nature — was not blessed or burdened with this virtue. That Mom's family tolerated him at all was a miracle, and probably due to pity and love for Mom and her brood.

At any rate they piled into the wagon and, pulled by the burros, left the desert and moved into Glendale. There they pitched tents on property owned by Aunt Hattie, and Robert and Ann started school locally.

Before long they were relocating once again, this time to Phoenix. Here Mom gave birth in October 1922 to another boy. This was George Warren, nicknamed 'Red.' He was a fiery, red haired, independent soul with a temper to match his hair, as everyone would find out in time. The children were enrolled in another school, but yet again didn't have time to settle. They must have been terribly confused to learn that the family was uprooting and off to the far west side of the city.

At least this house had a couple of relatively modern conveniences compared to what they were used to. Their two-room home came complete with a bath and an out-house with a flush toilet.

Unbelievably though, they scarcely had time to enjoy these luxuries before it was time to head for new pastures. This was probably because the rent was due. Dad did have 'taking' ways, and this may have had something to do with the frequent moves, especially as they occurred mostly at night. I can see where a car with no headlights would be a definite advantage.

They took the road to Tucson this time, traveling — so the story goes — in another Model T with no top during a hard rain storm. By this time Mom must have been numb and resigned to whatever lay ahead of her. She had to be torn between love and caring for her children and blind loyalty to her husband. Although I will never understand it, I can sympathize.

She must have decided it was a waste of effort to check the kids into school. If so, her hunch was right; the stay in Tucson was a short one. For reasons known only to himself, Dad loaded them all up again and headed for Benson, a small town about 50 hard (weren't they all?) miles southeast of Tucson.

There he found an abandoned farm house on acreage planted in corn. Since no one attempted to make them move on, they must have thought this might be a chance to settle for a little while.

Lillie was six years old and ready to start school. She and Pat and Ann rode the bus to school, and the family stayed put long enough for them to finish one term before being uprooted again.

As later recounted by Ann, Dad had butchered someone's cow without asking permission and I suppose he was afraid of the same fate. So he decided when the sun went down he would get on his way.

Heading back to Phoenix, they chanced upon another farm property that looked abandoned about midway through their journey. This was in the town of Florence. It seemed a good prospect for a family in search of shelter, particularly as there was a school within a convenient distance.

Even the news that the farm wasn't really abandoned proved to be only a temporary setback. The owners gave them permission to stay, and they settled down to life amid cows, chickens and fruit trees. With a bus to take them to school, the kids adapted quickly and there were passing report cards for Lillie, Pat and Ann at the end of term.

With that in mind, you'd think stability would have been a family priority. But no, they were off before the three kids had a chance for a second success. Why they left Florence I never learned, but I can only guess Dad felt the need to make himself scarce yet again. Could it be that the proximity of the State Penitentiary had some psychological bearing on his decision? It's just a thought.

Notes

[1] Apparently Gillett was erased from the map quite a few years ago. The site was west of I-17, near New River. According to Byrd Howell Granger's *Arizona's Names*, the settlement took its handle from D.B.Gillett, superintendent of the nearby Tiptop Mine.

Chapter Five
Birth of Twins

Driven by the desire to get far away from whatever or whomever was the current threat, Dad headed to the far west side of the valley. Home became a two-room house eight miles north of the small town of Glendale and near the Arizona Canal. Back then the road was known as Lateral 18; now it's 59th Avenue.[1]

It was here that Mom gave birth again, this time delivering twins on September 26th 1925. Gramma Heckle was living in Glendale at that time, and she was near enough to assist a Doctor Ross Martin at the birth. First to arrive, at 9:55 pm, was a boy, followed by a girl five minutes later. The boy was named Martin David after two uncles and the girl was named Mamie Ellen after two aunts.

My sister Lillie tells how, when she saw us for the first time and found that one of her new siblings was a boy, she covered his head because she did not want another brother. She was only seven years old, and had not known that Mom was going to have a baby. She was glad, at least, that there was a girl baby for her to play mother to.

There were lots of twins on both sides of the family, so I don't imagine this event caused much of a stir among the adults. Personally, I would have been very sick about it if I had been one of the adults, given our family's poor circumstances.

Martin was born with a bad case of a skin rash called eczema, which was cleared up in time with the medicine of the day. I'm told it was quite a common condition for newborns then, but have never been told why. He also had a badly twisted left ankle, probably caused either by the position in the womb or the manner of delivery. That too, straightened up with time, although he was badly bowlegged for many years and self-conscious about his legs all his life. It didn't stop him growing up to be a fast runner though.

As remembered by my sisters Ann and Lillie, the family's next relocation came when Martin and I were about eight months old.

Once more Dad was having to make himself scarce. He had stolen a Model T and had it hidden in back of the house. The Sheriff or a deputy had come to arrest him. But, not having a warrant to search the premises, the officer returned to Glendale to get one.

While they were gone he quickly loaded everyone in the car or truck — I think it was a truck — and drove out the back way, running over fences and ditches. The family took off up the Black Canyon Highway, which at that time was a narrow, mountainous, two-lane road running upstate from the Phoenix area.

I don't know how far he had gone before he got stuck in a deep gulch. Someone got word to Uncle Mart, and he brought his team of mules or horses and pulled the truck out.

The family went north again, this time to a ranch belonging to the Love family. It was situated near the Agua Fria River, somewhere around the hamlet of Humboldt, in the general direction of Prescott.

To the kids at least, the ranch was a real paradise. There was a big house surrounded by apple, peach and cherry trees. There were also horses to ride and milk cows.

For adults and kids alike, there must have been plenty of work to do as well. They went into the hills and caught a burro to hitch to an old plow that was on the property. The uneven match between burro and kids resulted in failure as far as doing any plowing, but provided much fun in the process.

Typically for this family, paradise didn't come without a hitch. The problem here was the lack of a school in the area. They were forced to move to a district providing one. Apparently they didn't have to travel far this time. They found what they were looking for at a small crossroads settlement centered on a post office, service station and store. The school was about a mile's walk from home.

(Mamie and her sisters made no mention of what 'home' was like here. It hardly mattered, in any case. This was another home that only lasted the length of a school term.)

Johnny was old enough to start school here, but he was very small for his age and the school did not want to enroll him. To add to school officials' reluctance, Johnny had been born a Maczinski in Michigan and his birth certificate was in that name. Ann had to vouch that he actually was a member of the Robinson clan.

Just before school was out they had to leave this lush, cool paradise, with all of the livestock that had become their friends and playmates, and head for the hot Salt River valley.

In a Model T Ford truck with no top and again with no lights — they must have been cheaper if they had no lights — they started out on the Black Canyon Highway again. Back then the highway was nothing like today's Interstate 17. The road was a narrow, winding trail, cut out of the rocks on the steep hills descending to the desert.

In many places Mom would make the kids get out and walk because of the danger. She was probably just as scared as the kids. I don't remember if she let Martin and I walk with the older kids or left us in the car.

We were almost four by this time and, though things are vague, I remember a stop for a few days under a huge tree with branches hanging down so far to the ground and so thick and dense that it was almost like one big room. The truck had broken down, I believe, and we had to stay here while it was fixed. It must have been like something out of *The Grapes of Wrath*.

In no time at all the tree became our home, with stove set up and lanterns placed around for light. Mom started the cooking and we were all getting ready to relax for the night. I remember plenty of canvas cots all over the place, inside our 'room' and outside.

48

All of a sudden the rains came. One of the desert's little surprises, this storm seemed to come out of nowhere and was as unwelcome as ants at a picnic.

By this time I was enjoying everything about this play house, so I was real surprised when the 'roof' leaked and everything and everyone began to get a soaking. There was a mad scramble to salvage the food and bed clothing before they were completely ruined.

Dad quickly stretched a tarp over the back of the truck. We threw everything under it, jumped in and all huddled together. I remember thinking how much fun this was. I don't remember what the food was but we ate it in the back of the truck. Eventually the rains stopped of course, and we cautiously moved out of the truck and back to our camp.

We must have stayed there for a few days to rest up for the next leg of the journey. We were not far from Cave Creek Dam and also a mine, remembered by the family only as 'Jack White's mine,' where Dad had planned on getting a job.

Aunt Hattie and Uncle George were living there, although I'm not sure if they were homesteading or working at the mine. However, Dad went to work there and Mom cooked for the miners. Even though this period immediately followed the rain storm that left such a vivid impression, I don't recall anything about it. I guess a child's memory can be very selective.

Dad's job at the mine must have been no more appealing than earlier situations. Before long we moved to a place near where we were born north of Glendale. We stayed put long enough for Lillie, Johnny, and Red to enroll in a one room school house there. Ann never went back to school again after we left the Prescott area.

After a few months it was on to Phoenix. As Ann tells it, we lived at 1701 East Madison, in a tent and a shack made out of Coca Cola signs.

. As far as I recall, that was the first time we attended a real church. Martin soon was delighted to find he had an attentive audience here for his singing and harmonica playing.

The church was called the Open Door Mission, at 17th Street and Washington, and was housed in a large tent. What made a big impression on me was the sawdust that covered the floor. I was nearly always bare foot, and remember how good it felt to squish my feet in it.

I liked going to church because all of the family went, even Dad. We all would sing and be on our 'good' behavior — sort of. Martin was shy at first, and would hide behind a door. But the offer of a nickel or dime would coax him into the open.

One time when he received a dime and a nickel, I remember, he was asked if he would share with me. After a little consideration, he decided to give me the dime because it was smaller.

I was always in his shadow, but that suited me just fine. Whatever good happened to him made me just as happy as it did him. We were always together, making our own conversation and good times. He was Mother's favorite, also Dad's, but I honestly never minded or resented it — just as long as I was included in all the attention he got.

We would argue of course, but I can't remember very many disagreements or even what the few we did have were about. The one advantage I did have was that I was bigger than Martin, and so when we wrestled I could always make him yell 'quits' first. Naturally, he couldn't stand this, and so was continually trying to get the better of me.

True to character, Martin had firm opinions about which food he liked and disliked. One food that he wouldn't eat no matter how Mom prepared it was onions. Once though, he was persuaded to try. Mom told him if he would eat his onions he'd grow as tall as me. He dived into the onions, but the result was not quite what Mom wanted. Martin quickly turned green and said: "I have to vomit." No one believed him — until he did.

He had a passion for milk, and one of our neighbors had cause to regret it. She was a nice lady, and so we were at her house a lot. One day she had a can of evaporated milk on her table. Martin told her to put it away, but she didn't listen. When she left us alone for a minute or two, Martin got on the table and drank the milk. I had nothing to do with this. I knew he was going to get in trouble, so I told on him.

Of course, the lady wanted to know why he'd done it. He'd told her to put it away, he answered, and she hadn't. So he had to drink it. I guess it made perfect sense to him, if not to her.

It was at this location in Phoenix in June 1930 that we were blessed with two baby brothers, who were named Harley and Charley. However, my memories of the births are nil, so I would imagine that we were shipped away somewhere while this event was taking place.

51

We weren't too interested in them, in any case, because there were too many other things to do. Even though we were living in the city, Mom didn't worry too much about where we were and so we were able to roam. No one was afraid of anything bad happening to us, and we always came home to eat.

That we grew up as healthy as we did is a medical mystery. I have very few memories of us being sick. There were few visits to the doctor for Martin and me anyway. Though Martin was small and for years badly bow legged, he seemed to be healthy and he was certainly active.

We did have one medical emergency, however, when we were about eight or nine. Martin had a severe reaction after being stung by a scorpion. He went numb and was paralyzed, and Uncle Mart rushed him into Glendale for treatment. Martin lived to tell the tale, of course, and being him relished telling it in great detail.

I was stung by a scorpion only once, and it did not affect me as badly as it did Martin. So I did not have the 'fun experience' of being rushed into town.

As for other ailments, I had an unglamorous strep infection when we lived farther out in the desert. The doctor made a house call and swabbed my throat with some awful tasting stuff. Another time I had to have a boil lanced over my eye and I fainted in his office. Hardly anything to make conversation about, I thought. So I remained silent, feeling the sooner it was forgotten the better.

While we were living on East Madison Street in Phoenix, the circus came to town. On their way to where the big top had been pitched, the animals passed right by our home. We watched from the side of the street, so close we could almost reach out and touch them. To us it seemed as if we had front row seats for free, and that thrilled us to death. It was the nearest to an actual performance that kids from a poor family like ours could expect to get.

For weeks afterwards we pretended to be circus performers. We played animal trainer, clowns — that wasn't hard — and trapeze artists. We even made our dog wear dresses and hats, and tried to make him do tricks. His best trick was disappearing, if I remember correctly.

Knowing our family, perhaps it was to be expected that this enthusiasm for animals would lead us into a confrontation. On one occasion we found a turtle, and took it home for a pet. Were we surprised when a neighbor came to our door and said that we stole it.

I was embarrassed and scared, because he was angry and I thought we were going to go to jail. Martin didn't seem to be too upset about it though, and sassed the man. Then my father came to our rescue, telling the man to get off our property. All this over a turtle.

With or without animals to include in our games, Martin and I were quite able to entertain ourselves. There was a park close by where we lived, and we were quite happy to spend our time there wrestling on the grass. Other little kids played with us, but mostly we preferred our own company.

One exception to this was going to church, when — instead of running off by ourselves — we would dress in our best and be together as a family. Mom would dress Martin and me alike, sometimes both in dresses and sometimes both in coveralls or boys jeans.

We accepted this for a long time. Then, one day in church, we had on dresses and someone told Martin that's not what boys wore. I can vividly recall a terrible scene with my mother. He was taken out kicking and screaming, and refused to go back into church until his outfit was changed.

We weren't too far from home, so presumably he was taken back and dressed in clothes he considered more suitable. At any rate, he had calmed down by the time he was brought back into church, and even volunteered to sing.

Notes

[1] The Arizona Canal had 20 'laterals,' or feeder canals, set one mile apart from each other. These laterals carried water from the Arizona Canal to area farms and ranches.

Chapter Six
Home Life

Our baby brothers were about a year old when it came time for our next change of address. Maybe we had worn out our welcome in the neighborhood or perhaps Dad got one of his urges to move on again, but move we did.

We left the big city for the familiar sights and sounds of the desert, this time near Cactus.[1] Once again home was an abandoned shack. Our new neighborhood consisted of a few scattered shacks and trailers belonging to people needing the dry air for their health.

After Phoenix, with its rows of closely spaced lots, the desert seemed to go on forever. You'd think we'd have room to stretch out, but instead the house we were to live in was cramped for a family of our size. From a child's viewpoint though it seemed large enough. We were outside for much of the time anyway.

By this time, the older children were much more independent and ready to make their own way in the world. Our eldest sister Ann had gotten married and our eldest brother Pat had left home. But despite the absentees there were still beds all over the place, and what seemed like an army of bodies. It would have been very grim but for the vast, sparsely inhabited expanse all around us.

We had no close neighbors. The nearest store, at the small crossroads settlement of Cactus, was about three miles away and the school was six.

A trip to the store was like a picnic. We all piled into our old truck, which rattled and shuddered throughout the brief journey to our destination.

As we well knew, a piece of candy or gum would be the reward for being good in the car. The store owner would give each of us a piece, or maybe a cookie. We especially liked a root beer flavored candy in the shape of a barrel. You can bet we were on our good behavior by the time we arrived.

Though wild and unruly most of the time at home, we knew where to draw the line. Dad was a stern, impatient person and would not hesitate to take the belt to any one of us he thought deserved it. He was not fair in any sense of the word. So a whipping mostly depended on his mood at the time — or whoever was the closest to him.

I was always in terrible fear of him, although I remember him hitting me only once — and that was only a light tap on the rear. It terrified me nonetheless, and I tried to stay out of his reach.

For the most part I went unnoticed by him. But I never got over my fear of his temper tantrums, when he would throw hammers or whatever else he had in his hand.

I sensed that my mother was afraid of him too, and so I kept a close eye on the situation. Dad drank a lot, and when he drank he was either very happy or very violent. We all walked softly until we knew his mood.

When he was in a good mood he would dance the Polish dances, sing Polish songs and put on a pretty good show for us. He could play the harmonica really well, and do a little fiddling too. His singing voice was good, as I remember it, or maybe it was just loud. For a small man, he made a lot of noise with his gruff voice. That could have been partly why I was so afraid of him, thinking back.

Dad's drinking must have had much to do with our frequent moves. When he did work he would put his back into it, and he did have skill as a mechanic. But most of the jobs he did have were manual labor because he was simply not stable enough to keep a good job for very long.

When we lived near Cactus, he used his truck to operate a garbage collection service. His route ran through the affluent Phoenix district surrounding the Biltmore Resort hotel, and his customers were very generous about giving him toys, clothes and other items for which they no longer had a need. These were always welcome treats, but the treat we looked forward to the most came on the days when a bakery would send boxes and boxes of donuts, sweet rolls and cakes.

Dad also had built pens for pigs, and began boarding and taking care of about 50 hogs and sows. They were fed on the garbage he collected. It was a lot of work for Dad and the older kids, but we younger ones had fun with the baby pigs. (Lillie had a lamb too, which ended up on the dinner table. Only the very hungry ate that night, as I recall.)

The arrangement was good, and Dad worked really hard on keeping the system running smoothly. Apart from the garbage route and. the pigs, we also had our own chickens and cows to supply us with fresh eggs and milk.[2]

Wild rabbits were plentiful and Mom became a crack shot with the shotgun, sometimes killing two with one shot. She was hard to live with when that happened. She would go out early to the field to bring in the cows to milk, and she always returned with two or three young rabbits or doves or quail. She made the best rabbit stew. We didn't have to be called twice at meal times.

The older boys easily could have gone to get the cows. But, as I look back, I realize she enjoyed this time by herself and would not have had it any other way.

She liked the open fields in the early morning, and perhaps dreamed the dreams she had before her life turned into the ugliness of a life with too many kids to feed, no house in which to live, and a very unreliable husband.

One of the few mechanical sources of entertainment available to us was an old wind-up Victrola record player. We had some records of Jimmie Rodgers and other singers of the day. Mom loved to put them on and listen while she fixed dinner. Martin would sing along, and she was so proud of him. One song I particularly remember was (Rodgers' 1929 recording) "All Around The Water Tank, Waiting For A Train."

Mom was not musical like Dad, but I know she liked to listen and even make an attempt to play her part. But she couldn't sing; she literally couldn't carry a tune. In spite of this she hummed a tuneless sound continually. Even as kids we were driven crazy by it! Not that there was much to sing about in her daily life. She worked so hard.

We were too small to do many chores. Harley and Charley were two years old, and Martin and I were not much bigger. We were a little more capable than our younger brothers though. One of our tasks was to gather wood for the stove. Although the desert had few large trees, there was a plentiful supply of mesquite, palo verde and ribs of dead saguaro cactus.

We also picked wild mustard greens which we found in the vicinity of the house, carrying our load back to the kitchen in a large pan. We never considered these chores because we had so much fun doing them. Much like Mom did going after the cows, I would imagine.

At that stage in our lives we — the children, that is — didn't think of ourselves as poor, even though we would get hungry and sometimes very cold and maybe want candy that we didn't have enough money to buy. Our father's drinking binges seemed to be the only fly in the ointment at this time.

The same determination to make the best of what we had available extended even to Christmas time. With no money for a tree, we searched the desert for a creosote bush in the shape of a pine tree. We returned home with the finest specimen we could find. Mom brought out the decorations, and we did all we could to make this scraggy desert plant look festive. It wasn't long till we had the spirit of the season.

There were not many presents to go around when the festivities arrived. But each of us would always receive one toy, and the rest of the gifts would be badly needed clothing. We opened all of them with the same excitement.

One year — I can't remember where we were living then — there was no money for any gifts at all. My mother, bless her, had each of us paint and fix up toys we already had and then wrap them in paper she had saved from the year before. She put our names on the packages and put them under the tree the night before Christmas. None of us knew what we were getting exactly but only that we got to open a package each. I can't remember if I was disappointed or not when it came time to unwrap.

Notes

[1] There have been several places in Arizona named for the abundance of cacti in their locality. This one, long since surrounded by the big city, was about 12 miles north of downtown Phoenix, around where Thunderbird Road now meets Cave Creek Road. Like the district of Sunnyslope to its south, Cactus was known — when Marty and Mamie were growing up — for its population of sufferers from tuberculosis and asthma.

[2] In Marty's mind, perhaps more so than Mamie's, this was a turning point in their lives. The family was comparatively well off in this period, Marty said in an interview, and their father owned three trucks besides the garbage collection business and hog raising. Only later, when their father indulged in too much drinking, did things go downhill. *The Nashville Tennessean*, October 10th, 1971.

Marty admitted to having his own drinking problems early in his career, and apparently it was his own role as a father that caused him to quit. When his son Ronnie became sick as a small child, Marty prayed he would recover and promised to stop drinking if he did.

Chapter Seven
School Age Brings More Independence

In 1931 the time came for these twin free spirits of the desert to go to school. New clothes came from somewhere. I remember them well. But they didn't make me any happier to leave the freedom of the open spaces.

We rode the bus for the first time in our lives, and I cried and sucked my thumb all that first day. I wanted to sit next to Martin, and for a while he and the teacher complied.

Finally Martin became disgusted with me. I wouldn't stop crying, and so he asked to be moved. The teacher put me beside my sister Lillie. Luckily for me, the two-room school house was shared by grades one to eight. So Lillie could not escape from her little sister.

Right away Martin began to make friends, and I saw soon enough that I was going to be left behind if I was not careful. Either I had to join in or I would lose him for sure. Eventually I adjusted, and learned to like school and having other girls to play with. The thumb-sucking continued for a while though. In spite of every effort to break me of it, I would manage to get that thumb into my mouth.

Mom tried and tried to get me to stop. When I was very small, she would put pepper on my thumb. But Martin, protective even at that age, would lick the pepper off. He would cry, and I would wonder why. Another method Mom tried was to tie my hand up. But Martin would untie me. She even tried putting a sock on my hand. Once again Martin came to the rescue. Spankings didn't stop me either. It was a long time before I quit the habit. I can't remember how, when or why I quit. But I do remember being embarrassed about it, because everyone made such fun of me.

We hadn't been at school long when we moved again. Fortunately, it was not a disruptive move. We were still in Cactus, and in fact were now much nearer to the school, which was by the way named Sunnyside School and was where we spent first and second grade.[1]

By midterm first grade we had become involved in school activities. Our house was maybe about the equivalent of two city blocks from the school. So it was easy to get to school plays and parties, and we didn't have to worry about whether Dad would be home to take us.

Although we all participated in the school plays, Martin was always the most eager. During one play, he was dressed as a package and had to sing a little verse. This was right up his alley and he gave it all he had. I played the part of a housemaid, and I thought I was pretty good too. But Martin got all the attention. That has never been very hard to figure out certainly. Martin looked for attention, and thrived on it.

I still looked forward to the end of the school day, when we could run home, change clothes and be out in the open again. We would hurry through whatever chores Mom had given us and be on our way.

My eagerness to finish formal lessons did not mean we had no more interest in school however. Quite the opposite as it turned out. We lived so close to the school that it became a prime target for our exploring nature.

There were no neighbors around and, once evening came, no one at the school either. The temptation to investigate further was too much, and Martin discovered that he could open a window. Naturally his next thought was to take a look inside.

I was so scared at first that I wanted to go back home. But I was talked into going through the open window and, with a boost from Martin, that's what I did.

Once we were both in, I lost my fear and followed him around. We went through the teacher's desk, and anything else that wasn't locked.

Initial curiosity satisfied, Martin turned his attention to the school's collection of musical instruments. He became a one-man band, trying everything he could find. He must have felt as if he had died and gone to Heaven he was having so much fun.

First the xylophone. I looked on in awe as he actually played some tunes. Then Martin moved on to the piano, where he worked out some more songs while I was trying desperately hard to wrestle "God Bless America" out of the xylophone. I never made it as a musician, but it didn't discourage me as a willing partner in crime.

The next day I was so scared and felt so guilty. I just knew that any minute the teacher would confront us with our break-in. I'm sure that Martin could not think of anything else that day either. The difference, I'm sure, was that he could not wait to try it again. He was on to something good and knew it. The fact that he had got away with it made it even better. From then on, our evening escapades at the school were a regular happening.

No one — not even brothers, sisters, mother or father — ever found out about it. Of course the school didn't either, or our adventure would have been very short-lived.

We never stole anything. Martin just played all of the instruments, and I sat and listened. I probably applauded, but I don't remember. I was so proud of him. He seemed so amazing to me, being able to sit down and get tunes out of those instruments. But I couldn't tell anyone about it.

About this time, the Shriners treated the school to the circus. We could hardly believe that we were actually going to see the same animals that we had seen a few years before go right by our house. But we did, and we walked on air for days afterwards. What a fun day — candy, popcorn, balloons, the works — and we didn't have to worry about our dad getting drunk and ruining it for us.

The next year the circus came again. I never forgot how exciting it was, and always wanted to see another one. Finally I did, many, many, years later, and it was just as exciting. I meant to ask Martin if he ever went again, but it always escaped my mind.

The Shriners also gave a case of Coca-Cola to anyone in the class who got all 'A's on their report card. Our kind teacher gave all the students 'A's, and since there were four Robinsons in the school we made quite a haul. Remembering too well the root beer caper, we watched Martin closely to see he didn't go near the hammer and nails.

This must have been just before a school holiday, because we put the cases of Coca-Cola and some food in the old truck and went to a family get together. Our destination was Uncle Mart and Aunt Ellen's place, over on the far north side of Glendale near the canal bank. All the cousins, aunts and uncles who could make the trip would be there.

We were so happy to be going somewhere all together, and finally to be able to drink our stash of Cokes and have such an assortment to eat. Most of all, we were eager to see our cousins and to run around in an unfamiliar area.

The truck chugged into our uncle's yard. We jumped from the back as the truck was still moving, and into the arms of our equally excited cousins, the Sullivans.

I was only too happy to release my obsession with my brother to play some real girl games with my favorite cousin, Lois. She was a few months younger than me. But we had the same problem — too many brothers.

Smugly we showed our cousins our contribution to the festivities, the packs of Cokes, adding that they could not have any until we had iced them down. I can still see the wash tub full of ice and all those beautiful bottles of Coke floating in it. What fun it was!

The boys disappeared into the undergrowth on their way to the canal to go swimming, mercifully leaving Lois and me to our dolls and other sissy and silly things that girls do.

All the kids were so engrossed in their own pursuit of entertainment, completely oblivious to the adults. None of us saw the signs of what was going to ruin our visit that day and cloud the family atmosphere for days to come.

Somehow, somewhere, Dad got hold of a bottle of whiskey. Instead of getting 'happy drunk' he got 'mean drunk,' and something set off his temper. Perhaps somebody said the wrong thing to him, or maybe Mom asked the impossible — "Please don't drink any more."

Whatever it was, his return to insanity caused him to tell us all to get back into the truck, and straightaway we started back across the desert to home. He would not wait even for us to pick up a few of our Cokes.

Such was our fear of him when he was in this condition that we did not protest, or even cry. I'm sure that mine was not the only sick stomach.

It was a sad, scared bunch of 'desert rats' that got out of the truck when we reached home. The incident was never mentioned again, and life resumed as usual.

That occasion was only one of many. Seldom did a day of fun begin and end without this kind of disappointment. It was one reason why we were satisfied with the desert and our own company. We rarely had visitors. But, never knowing how our dad was going to behave, we didn't mind.

Our house in Cactus was as nice a home as any we ever had. Really it was the only nice one. All the same, it was very modest by today's standards.

The furniture was sparse to non-existent. There was just a table from which to eat, and a chair or two and wooden boxes on which to sit. In one corner of the kitchen was our big, cast-iron stove. The living room was large, and had beds all around it — like a bunkhouse.

We had acquired a battery-operated radio, but only played it at night when everyone was home so we could save the batteries.

These were times I liked, although I never joined Dad and Martin in singing along to the radio. I must have been born shy and insecure. I surely did like the music. But I could never get up the nerve to join in, and no one ever asked me.

I felt terribly unloved by everyone but Martin. He rarely left me out of anything. But in this case he probably felt it wasn't his show. Or then again, maybe he realized I couldn't sing.

Martin's knack of making me feel wanted extended to school too. After getting over the initial feelings of newness, I never felt left out. In fact, in a way school seemed like an extension of home, with so many of us from the same family in the same building.

But my contentment didn't last long. Not for the first or the last time, our lives were disrupted by the news we were about to move. I was brokenhearted. Martin and I went on our last trip through the school window. We looked around the room at all the lovely musical instruments and felt like our world had come to an end.

We didn't know where we were moving. No one felt it was important enough to tell us, or perhaps they didn't know themselves.

Quiet, confused and scared, we walked the quarter of a mile home, forfeiting our usual foot race — which Martin always won.

It was dark by this time, and the family possessions were piled on the truck and blankets placed so that we could sleep on the way to who knew where. With familiar knots in our stomachs, we curled up beside each other and went to sleep.

I remember feeling so sad for Martin because he would not be able to sneak into school and play the piano again. Even then I knew I never wanted to be away from him. Although he could do nothing about our situation, he represented safety to me, and as long as he was close by I didn't care where we lived.

I'll never forget the happiness I felt when the old truck rattled to a stop in front of an empty house. This was to be our new home, and it was only about half a mile from my favorite uncle and aunt, Mart and Ellen, and my neat cousin Lois. Martin and I looked at each other in sheer delight. We were still in the desert we loved so much. I was so happy to see him smiling and acting crazy again.

It didn't take us long to start exploring. This time we had some guides — our cousins Dick, Jim, Lois and little Annie (not to be confused with my big sister, Ann).

Home was now only about a mile from the house where Martin and I were born, and not too far from the canal.

Dad and the boys built chicken pens, a new outhouse, and a small house of sorts for Dad to sleep in. A milking stall was built for the cow, and we were in business. Mom could, and did, continue shooting rabbits early in the morning when she brought in the cow. A mile or so away was Mr. Dillard's citrus grove, which in season provided our supply of vitamin C.

Martin's musical talents continued to develop. He was hardly ever without his harmonica, and was encouraged by Uncle Mart, who played fiddle and loved to have Martin play along with him on harmonica.

Aunt Ellen was my refuge and confidante, one I could go to and receive the love and attention I wanted so badly from my mother. Mom had no time for me, and at times didn't even seem to like me at all. I'm sure she did really, but her time was so consumed coping with her large brood and her husband.

For the boys, the canal became a center of activities. They spent their summer days swimming, hunting rabbits, catching small desert ground squirrels and making pets of them.

With so many other kids around, Martin and I began to go our different ways more often here. We still had our private times together though, when we would talk about what we would do when we grew up.

My dream was to have a big house with a sofa. To me, a sofa was the epitome of rich living. I don't know why. Martin didn't seem to care much about that or think it was a great thing.

He was still a prankster at heart. One time he was watching from the brush on the edge of the canal while a couple went skinny dipping. He stole their clothes and hid them and came home calmly for dinner. Not long after we had sat down to eat, a very angry man came to the door demanding to know who had taken their clothes. No one even suspected that Martin had done it. But he quickly disappeared and returned with the clothes. The 'brat' was still only eight years old, but even then he could not resist a good practical joke.

As summer progressed the newness of having a lot of kids to play with wore off, and Martin and I began to miss our own private treks into the desert. We discovered that if we got up really early we could be gone before anyone missed us.

Whatever we could find in the kitchen that wasn't under lock and key we took with us. Sometimes it would be a couple of potatoes. We took some matches — a real no-no — and far from the house we dug a hole, buried the potatoes in coals, covered them with dirt, and let them bake while we went on our way. Later we returned and ate them. It was a risky method of cooking. Sometimes we didn't time our trips too well and they were burned black when we uncovered them. Other times they were not done well enough, but we ate them anyway.

One of our pastimes was looking for scorpions, snakes and other varmints of the desert. I wasn't afraid when I found a scorpion, but a snake would petrify me. Martin would stand and throw rocks at one until he killed it.

Cow chips were all over the desert, and under each one would be three or four scorpions. After a while we lost count of who killed the most.

Lost in our own world, we would not get home sometimes until after dark. No one ever seemed worried — a chilling thought now, but then hardly anything to raise an eyebrow. That anyone would harm a couple of young children playing in the desert seemed unthinkable.

This, for us, was freedom. Freedom from the bickering and quarreling that seemed to be endless at home.

We worried about our mom all the time, because we were beginning to realize that the things she put up with were not right.

Our dad's drinking and cruelty to her and the older boys bothered us more and more, although we didn't have any idea what to do about it. We would talk about growing up and marrying each other and taking care of Mom. At 45 she seemed very old to us, and we were afraid she was going to die. We thought we saw little signs that she was failing. If she didn't answer us, for instance, we thought she was going deaf and would signal to that effect when she wasn't looking.

We became consumed with fear for her, and convinced that we were going to lose her in some way. Small wonder we spent so much time in the open spaces where we could find a measure of freedom from such concerns.

As an alternative to the desert, sometimes we headed for the citrus grove and played there instead. I'm sure our conversations were deep and interesting, and I would like to recount each and every one. But the truth is I remember very few clearly enough to do that. So you will have to take my word for it.

Living so close to the canal, we spent a lot of time in the water. Quite apart from the canal, there were also many irrigation ditches in the area.

The boys all learned to be good swimmers, and I had every intention of doing the same. However, when I realized that they were determined to drown me, I confined my paddling to the ditches, which were shallower than the canal. Even there, I wasn't entirely safe. But it was easier to get out of a ditch than the canal. As a result though, I've never been comfortable in the water and never learned to swim. At age 30 I took swimming lessons, but never got over the fear of drowning.

Inevitably, this period of leisure had to come to an end. Just as we were growing accustomed to our new surroundings and companions, it was time to enroll in school again.

Notes
[1] Opened in 1930, Sunnyside Elementary later became Greenway Middle School, located at 3002 E. Nisbet.

Chapter Eight
A Born Entertainer

Our change in residence meant that we would be enrolling in a new school. This was not something I wanted to think about. It had been an effort for me to find my niche at Sunnyside, and now I was being forced to deal with new faces.

Such was my reluctance to face this new school that, given the choice, I would happily have agreed to stay at home for the rest of my life. Although the situation there was not ideal, it seemed the lesser of two evils at the time.

As before, new clothes arrived from somewhere. This time I think Uncle Mart bought them. Sometimes clothes may have come from the county, because we always had new ones at the start of the school year even when we had no money to buy them. I can remember the smell of newness they had, although it wasn't long before they began to look worn and old.

We were starting the third grade at this time, and living in the Peoria School District. We walked about half a mile to catch the bus, and it seemed we rode a long way to Peoria.

While I cowered in my seat, Martin immediately made friends with everyone on the bus, including the driver.

A little girl named Nancy came over to me and asked me my name. I told her it was Mamie and she laughed and laughed, saying it was the funniest name she had ever heard. I happened to agree with her, but nevertheless I started to cry. Later she became my best friend during the years we went to Peoria School.

All the same, I smarted over her remark all through morning classes and was still upset at recess time. I stood by myself in the corner of the school grounds, not attempting to make friends and no doubt feeling sorry for myself.

Martin was having such fun with all the other kids. Finally he looked my way and came over. He stood with me for a while. But he couldn't understand why I would be upset about such a seemingly insignificant thing as Nancy's remark about my name. Eventually he eased away from me, and was on his way back to the center of activity. I knew once again that I would have to shape up or risk losing Martin's respect.

I really didn't want to play with the boys. Luckily, Nancy must have been feeling sorry for what she had said, for she came over and asked me if I want to play. Of course I did, and from then on everything at school was all right.

The teacher's name was Mrs. Sharp. The name described her personality very well. I don't remember her as a very nice teacher.

She had no patience with Martin and his antics. It didn't seem to bother him very much, although I cried a lot when she would spank his hand with a ruler. It was not so hard to understand her impatience with him though. He was never still, and frequently talked in class.

Mrs. Sharp resorted to putting Scotch tape over his mouth to keep him quiet. She knew she wasn't going to call on him for answers. His total lack of concentration for anything academic kept him in constant trouble in the classroom. None of it was of a very serious nature, although at the time it seemed so to me.

It was a different story though when it came time to put on classroom plays. When Mrs. Sharp picked students for the various parts, she invariably chose Martin for one of the more important roles. If not the hero, it was something equally prominent.

Martin had to struggle with the three 'R's, it was true. But he did his best to make up for academic shortcomings in other activities.

He excelled, for instance, in playing ball of any kind. If a touch football or baseball game was being organized, he would be the first one chosen for a team. We were both good at track. Martin said it was from chasing jack rabbits.

He was continually challenging other boys to wrestling matches, as if he had to prove that being small was not a handicap. For him it wasn't, because he seldom lost a match. Even when he did lose, he would hold no grudge and smile or laugh like it was no big deal.

He would love to tease my friends and me when we were playing. He would seem to appear from nowhere, and do something dumb like take whatever we were playing with and run away with it. He knew we wouldn't catch him, and he just waited for us to give up. To add insult to injury, he made up nicknames for everyone and would use them to mock our efforts to reach him.

He would go from one piece of mischief to another. At times like these, I would get so mad at him because it was so hard to excuse his behavior to my friends. They thought he was terrible, and I had to agree. He was never cruel or mean — just a brother, I guess.

Home life remained much the same though. When we got off the bus at the bridge across the canal, we seldom went right home. A short run along the canal bank and through the thickets of mesquite trees surrounding the house got us in good shape for the evening meal.

Most of the hard chores were left for our older brothers. We would feed the chickens or clean the rabbit pens and sometimes take our little brothers for hikes, scaring them to death with wild stories about snakes and other perils of the desert.

We had a sneaky way of making sure our brothers didn't make these walks go on too long. Not too far away lived another family. We told Harley and Charley that this family included a crazy person who had to be tied to a tree. The idea worked very well, and we never had to take them far from our house. I guess it was unkind to spin this yarn really, but they really did slow us down.

Martin must have started feeling the same way about me in fifth and sixth grades, because our paths separated to an extent at that time. We were in the same classes. But it was an age at which boys tended to do one set of things and girls another, and there wasn't so much contact between us as there had been. Anyway, Martin teased my friends and me far too much for me to want him around.

By the fourth grade the students were in the habit of walking to Peoria's main street and getting into a little mischief. It was only a block from the school, and there was a grocery store, a drug store, one for hardware, and several others.

The boys were always stealing candy, gum and other small items from the drug store. The man who ran the place never seemed to be around to wait on anyone, and it became so easy for the boys to steal that it was an everyday occurrence.

One day Martin and I were in the grocery store on the corner. Martin filled his pockets with loot and started to walk out. Before he could reach the door, the storekeeper came over to him, picked him up, turned him upside down and shook all the stolen articles out of his pockets.

I felt so humiliated. But Martin only laughed, and ran as fast as he could back to school. It was at times like this that I wasn't too proud of him, although I would never have told anyone that — and certainly didn't want anyone else to say anything bad about him.

His best friend in these lower grades in Peoria was named Henry. Actually I'm not sure whether Martin truly considered Henry to be his best friend. But they were certainly together a lot. Like us, Henry was also a poor, ragged little kid, and the two boys may well have felt that the best way to survive was to hang together.

These were depression years for everyone, although at the time it seemed as if some were far richer than others in this farming community. It wasn't until years later that we found out that other families were just as doubtful about making it financially as we were.

Besides, riches are all a matter of how you see things. I thought my friend Nancy was really rich when I visited her and saw that she lived in a house that wasn't falling down, and that she had her own bedroom with pretty blankets and bedspreads.

Years later she told me she liked to visit me as a child because I had so much more to play with than she did. By that she meant spaces to roam, trees to climb, and the endless thickets that served us as imaginary rooms and houses in which to play.

Nancy was from a small family. She had one brother. I thought he was cruel and scary because he was a bully. On the school bus, he would take my nickel away from me. Not even Martin could help me get it back.

When we had no school, Nancy would often visit with me all day. She would arrive early in the morning and stay until her father came after her.

When she came to play, there would be a certain amount of jealous rivalry between my cousin Lois — another frequent playmate — and me. But in an effort to outfox Martin, the three of us would usually end up banding together and the visit would turn out well.

We had to watch continually for Martin and his tricks. Once I thought I had lost Nancy's friendship because of him. We were playing around a haystack. It seemed awfully high to me at the time, but in reality was probably only a few feet. Martin sneaked up on one side of it and jumped down on to us, taking us completely by surprise and scaring us badly in the bargain.

Nancy began crying and wanted to go home right then. She had no way of getting to her house, so instead she went with Lois to her home. I was sure I had lost my best friend, and was really upset with Martin. I began crying and chasing after him. He tried to say he was sorry for scaring us, but at that point it was too late for apologies.

Determined to get back in favor, Martin changed tactics and became very attentive and kind towards me. He was going to make me some soup, he said. I couldn't stay mad at him, so I accepted his offer. At that point I felt I had the upper hand because he was acting so sorry about what he had done.

He told me to stay outside and he would surprise me. I did as he said, and he brought me a clear, broth-like concoction in a big coffee mug. It didn't look like any soup I had ever seen before, but I took a big gulp of it anyway.

I should have known by this time that he wasn't to be trusted when he was that nice. The 'soup' turned out to be a cup of hot water heavily spiced with peppery Tabasco sauce.

Naturally there was a long chase, with the usual crying, screaming and rock throwing. But he had accomplished what he wanted, and that was to get rid of the other two girls so he could once more get his way. He didn't like to be ignored, and we had been doing a good job of ignoring him.

The rest of the day, while he was hiding from me, I schemed and plotted about how I would get even with him. I knew he would not eat anything that I offered him, so it had to be something really sneaky.

Just before bedtime, I poured a glass of water in his bed and he had to sleep on the very edge of the bed to keep dry. I had one eye open, you can be sure, until I knew he was asleep.

I didn't have his imagination for these devilish tricks, so they were always started by him and most often went unavenged. I think I kept hoping that some day he would find someone else who would be an easier target. He was never punished for any of these pranks, and no doubt I would not have liked it if he had been. For the most part I held my own, learning to hit and run.

I will say that he would never let anyone else do the things that he did to me. He would fight our elder brothers when they teased me. For a long time Red had a scar on his forehead where Martin threw a horseshoe at him when he was making me cry.

If I got a spanking for anything, Martin would come over to console and hug me. On these occasions I could forgive him easily for all his rotten tricks. He never hurt me physically, and it probably didn't occur to him that his tricks hurt me in any way either.

In school he pretty much left me alone. But even when his pranks were not directed at me, I couldn't help feeling involved. When he was antagonizing teachers and schoolmates, I had one eye on what Martin was doing. I was never able to help him, but I hurt inside when he was getting a lecture from the teacher. He never seemed to be bothered by any of it, and went on to the next bit of trouble.

In those days the teachers spanked hard, and it seemed he was constantly getting the paddle. There were times I could hardly stand it, and I couldn't understand how he could laugh about it. At home at night, I would tell Martin how I hated the teacher that whipped him. But he would say: "That didn't hurt at all."

Johnny and Red were always laughing at home about his troubles at school that day, and I would get very mad at them and tell them it wasn't his fault.

Defending Martin turned out to be a waste of energy on my part though. Mom and Dad didn't show much concern over him getting into trouble, and Martin showed no sign of changing his ways.

One of his stunts was to walk behind the teacher mimicking her walk and expressions until she turned around and saw him. Then there would follow the inevitable paddle. This continued throughout the elementary grades, and always brought the laughs from the other students that seemed to make the punishment worthwhile to him.

This devilish streak certainly must have puzzled teachers and others who came into contact with Martin, because alongside it ran a kind, caring aspect of his nature. The two were difficult to reconcile. Of course I knew there was a kind side to Martin, but even I could be taken by surprise when it appeared suddenly.

One day, in the third or fourth grade, Martin saw a little Mexican girl sitting on some steps eating her lunch. She was all by herself, and looked very lonesome. I remember she was eating a bean burro.

When Martin started walking in her direction, my heart stopped. I thought he was going to take her lunch from her. But all he did was sit down by her, take his ever-present harmonica out of his pocket and start playing for her, or perhaps I should say to her, because I'm not sure whether she welcomed it or not. If she felt like I did, she was relieved probably that he was not going to interfere with her lunch. I like to think that Martin just felt she needed some company.

Chapter Nine
Diverging Paths

It was inevitable, I suppose, that Martin and I could not share the same interests and activities forever. In some things I no longer kept up with him, and in others I didn't really want to take part at all.

Martin became quite a tree climber, and could go up the highest ones very fast. So good at this was he that people would call him a monkey. I would stand below and wish I could be up there too. But I rarely had the courage to try.

One time I did manage to get about six feet off the ground and was too afraid to look down, much less start the descent. I might be up there still if he hadn't taken pity on me and very carefully and kindly worked with me until I reached the ground.

He could at times be very patient with me and my crybaby ways, although he must have wished badly that I had been a boy. I was never a real tomboy. After a childhood of roughing it in the desert, I can't imagine why not.

But I stayed up with Martin as long as I didn't have to endanger my life in any way, like climbing trees or swimming the canal. These life-threatening things — as I saw them — I left to him. I wanted the ground under my feet at all times.

When I did join in with one of his escapades, against my better judgment, I often came to regret it. The tree climbing was one example. But there was another, with more lethal consequences.

Martin made me a type of slingshot, using strips of inner tube and a forked tree branch. A rock was placed in a pocket in the rubber strip. The pocket was pulled back, let go, and the rock flew on its course. Much depended, of course, on the aim and strength of the shooter.

With this weapon we went hunting. Not too far from the house, we spotted a little bird in a tree. Martin was ready to teach me how to use it.

I pulled back on the rubber strips as hard as I could, but the rock just fell at my feet. Several times I tried again, with the same result. The bird must have been feeling very safe, because it made no effort to fly away.

However, I sensed Martin's disgust with me, so the next time I gave it all I had. The rock flew fast and hard, hitting the bird and killing it.

I don't know what I had expected, but it wasn't this. I began to cry. I had never killed anything in my life, and I knew for sure that this time I was really going to go to Hell. I felt so sorry for what I had done, and wouldn't stop crying. Martin started crying too, and we decided to bury the bird and give it a funeral.

We had heard about funerals, but had never been to one. So we just did the best we could. First we dug a small hole. Then Martin went back to the house, and emptied and brought back a matchbox that was kept over the stove. The bird just fit inside the box, which we buried in the hole with its contents. Finally we put a stick on the grave so that we could find the site again.

From then on I decided that I would just be an observer, and let Martin do the shooting. Despite my lack of participation in these more adventurous exploits, Martin must have appreciated my role as an admiring observer because he seemed to want me around all the time in our early years.

We were growing up however, and Martin was beginning to spend more time with Johnny and Red. This wasn't always to his liking. The two older boys were much stiffer competition for him and didn't put up with his mischief, not thinking he was as funny as I did.

Harley and Charley were getting bigger too, but not big enough to argue with me when I wanted to play house and make them be my kids. I would dress Harley in girls' dresses because he had such a pretty face and was so little.

I would want Martin to belong to my play family. But as usual he made trouble, so I didn't ask him too often. It was rare for him to play an hour with us without harassing us so badly we would have to quit. He became so bossy and obnoxious sometimes that even I was ready to kill him.

Once, he gave Harley a dish of play food. All it was really was maize, kept to feed the chickens. What Harley didn't know was that there was an ant in it. The next thing we knew that ant had stung Harley on the tongue.

His tongue began to swell, and he was obviously in great pain. Even the effort to cry was difficult.

Instead of being sympathetic, Martin made fun of him, which just caused him to cry all the harder and look even funnier. I feel sorry even now for that and wonder how we could have been so cruel, because I laughed too.

Martin and I rarely fell out with each other. But as with any brother and sister, those occasions did arise.

Each of us kids had been given a baby turkey, and told to take very good care of it. Martin and I kept ours in a separate pen. One day I was running by the pen when I stumbled and landed on his turkey. I don't know how we determined it was his.

Anyway Martin became very angry and yelled at me, because the little creature was thrashing around dying. I was really scared about that, and wondered what Martin was going to do to me. He screamed out: "You cruel bitch." He had never sworn at me before. I was so confused I yelled back: "Don't call me cruel." At the time, I couldn't understand why everyone regarded this with such amusement. Everyone but him and me, that is.

We were fortunate in having our cousins nearby to play with and their home to give us a refuge when needed. It was lucky for us that they lived as close as they did. Many times we had to walk to their place to stay out of reach of a drunken, mean and dangerous father. When we would come home in the morning, he had no idea we had ever been gone.

Dear Aunt Ellen always found a bed for us in her already crowded house. I felt safe with our relatives, and most often did not want to go back home. Uncle Mart would play his fiddle for us all and it was like a party, except that we knew that Mom was back there with him and there was nothing we could do about it.

The babies, Harley and Charley, stayed with her of course. She said he did not bother her so badly if she was holding one or both of them. By this point, Harley and Charley were not really tiny babies. But they remained "the babies" to all of us. I don't remember our father being mean to the smaller children, including Martin and me.

It was amazing that he could be so happy and fun loving sometimes, and turn into a raging fool at other times. During his drunken periods, he would fly off at anyone close at hand. So we tried hard to stay out of his way.

We were all getting older, and it seemed that his drinking was getting worse. Or perhaps we just noticed it more. Small wonder that we preferred the desert and its unknown dangers to the ones we knew at home. One of his tantrums was enough to scare the daylights out of anyone.

Chapter Ten
Living in Tents

Once again we had to go through the uncertainty and anguish of moving to a new home. We were going only a short distance to the north west, so we would still be near our cousins and still in the Peoria school district. This time though, instead of a house, we were to live in tents. What prompted the move I never did know. But I certainly didn't like leaving the house.[1]

The two big tents seemed huge to me. They were set up facing each other, separated by what might be called a breeze way covered by a tarp.

One tent served as the kitchen, and contained the faithful old wood range as well as tables, whatever we used for chairs, and the usual cupboards for groceries.

The other tent was for the beds. Our two older brothers Johnny and Red slept on cots outside, and Mom, Martin, Harley, Charley and I slept inside. Dad had made himself a small one-room shed a short distance away from the tents, and that's where he slept.

Being the real little homemaker and the only girl by this time, as Annie and Lillie had both gotten married, I busied myself fixing up things as much as I could.

We hauled water in big barrels for drinking and bathing. And yes, a Saturday night bath was for real. The water was heated on the stove in pots. In winter we bathed in a washtub by the stove. In summer the boys used the canal, but Mom and I stuck with our tub.

Even though we used water sparingly, the insides of our tents were kept as clean as possible. I was being given a lot more chores by this time, and I learned to use the washboard and scrub clothes with bar soap. Like another chore I was given, washing dishes, it wasn't a very pleasant pastime. But that was how the work was divided.

While we were expected to do these chores as part of our family duty, we were allowed also to take on outside jobs. For these, we could save what we were paid.

It worked out better for the boys. They would sometimes go to work a few miles away at a citrus farm, owned by a Mr. Dillard. I was not allowed to go with them. So instead I would do little chores for Aunt Ellen. She didn't need my help, but she knew how much I wanted to earn some money like the boys. A dime was worth a lot back then.

One job that kept all the kids busy was collecting scrap brass, tin, copper and other pieces of metal for a junk man who came by every week. The city dump was a few miles north of us, and we would keep a watch for cars and trucks going past on their way to unload trash.

Martin and I, now joined by our two younger brothers Harley and Charley, would make our way out to the dump and go through the new find. Then we would drag home our wagon loaded with scrap. We each had our own pile of scrap, and the new load would be divided equally between the four of us. At least, that was the idea. But I had to keep a close eye on Martin to keep his pile from growing at the expense of mine.

When the junk man made his rounds and weighed our haul, we sometimes came out with two or three dollars each. We were rich. It was enough to buy plenty of ice cream and other goodies at school. Martin would use part of his share sometimes to see Gene Autry movies in Glendale.

There have been stories that say that Martin earned money from picking cotton around this time. But that was never the case.[2] Martin's money came from fruit picking and picking up scrap metal.

Apart from money, those citrus orchards gave us a ready supply of oranges and grapefruit. Mr. Dillard supplied us generously. He would come by in his truck and play a game of catch with us. He would throw the oranges and see if we could catch them. At least, I think that was why he threw them. He was such a nice man I can't believe he'd throw them intending to hit us. Sometimes he would leave a box of fruit for us. We would sit and eat our fill of the fruit, and then use the remainder for games of catch.

Even though we had all the oranges we could use, Martin couldn't resist seeing if we could sneak into the orchard and steal some from the trees. It wasn't much fun for me. I just knew Mr. Dillard was aware of what we were doing, and it made me feel so guilty. But I went along with Martin anyway.

Not all Martin's exploits were so successful though. Once he fell out of a tree and broke his wrist. That slowed him down some, and he had to stay home from school. I'm surprised there weren't more broken bones. But we were all pretty lucky in that respect.

One morning I went out to catch the school bus. But instead of getting on it, I sneaked back home to be with Martin, who was still recovering from his broken wrist. We spent the day playing out of sight of the house. Then, when the kids came home from school, I pretended I had been with them.

I really got into trouble when Mom found out from the school that I had not been there that day. I was excused for it later because, being a twin, people thought that I had had "sympathy pains." I don't remember having any, but I went along with the logic of it. Martin would "miss the bus" quite often and would get to stay at home. I was afraid to try it very often.

All of us were spending more and more time away from home, in large part because of Dad's drinking. Even when we did do something together, like go into town to see a movie, the likelihood was that Dad would get drunk and turn the trip into a nightmare for me.

The older boys and Martin were allowed to walk into town by themselves, but I could never go with them. I had to stay at home, and so did Harley and Charley. When we could, we kept our distance from the tents so we didn't have to hear our parents fighting.

Sometimes I would go to my friend Nancy's house, about five miles away, and play with her in peace. I would be given a ride over there, and we would play house or paddle in an irrigation ditch.

Even at these times, we did not escape entirely. Often Martin would show up and throw rocks at us. It seemed as if he came from nowhere. When we went after him, he ran away laughing like crazy.

Needless to say, Nancy didn't like him at all. Telling on him did no good, so we had to suffer. Mom definitely had a blind side when it came to Martin's tricks. The ditch, by the way, is still there. I think of us playing there every time I drive by it.

We were living on a pension of some sort that Dad was getting during this period. If Mom took us to the store, there was plenty to eat. But if Dad decided to go shopping when the pension money arrived, he never came home with much of it.

At one point, I remember, Christmas was coming. We were very sad because we thought there would be nothing for us. But on Christmas Day Dad had the biggest bunch of presents for us. There were dolls, wagons, clothes, toy cars, and candy of all kinds. He had kept them hidden in his little shack, which was off limits to everyone but him. What a wonderful day that was. We didn't know where he got the money for all these presents, and we never thought to ask. The day was over all too soon.

Our joy didn't last. Shortly afterwards Dad and Red got into a fight that caused Red to run away from home.

Whenever there was a fight between Dad and any of the boys or Mom, I just sort of disappeared. So the incident between Dad and Red is rather vague in my memory. They were eye to eye and threatening each other when Mom stepped between them. I was gone as fast as I could the half mile to Uncle Mart's. When I came back home much later, Red was gone. We seldom saw him again.[3]

Notes

[1] The tents were in the vicinity of 59th Avenue and Thunderbird, as far as Mamie could recall, so they were still close to where they had been born.

[2] This of course contradicts Marty's own accounts, given in interviews, in which he says he did pick cotton. The definitive bibliography of these interviews, if you can find a copy, is contained in Barbara J. Pruett's 1990 book *Marty Robbins: Fast Cars and Country Music* (The Scarecrow Press).

[3] Red was 14 years old at the time of this confrontation with their father. Apparently he was never an integral part of the family circle again. After years of little contact, Mamie said, Red showed up at a performance by Marty in Texas. What the two brothers had to say to each other would be interesting to know.

Chapter Eleven
Wrong Side of the Tracks

In January 1937 Mom took us kids to live in Glendale. We moved to a house that belonged to her mother, who by that time had died. I guess Mom had decided that it was way past time to get away from Dad. Uncle Mart helped the boys with the moving. Into his truck we put the trusty cast-iron stove and our other belongings and drove away, leaving the tents behind us. We must have been 12 at the time.

It was in Glendale that I first remember Martin picking up a guitar. Our eldest sister Ann had one that she wasn't making much headway on. Martin was soon picking out tunes on it of course. I think Ann showed him a couple of chords, but mostly he just sat and did it. Before long we were singing "You Are My Sunshine."[1]

Martin's progress on guitar was one of the few bright spots in our day to day lives. Looking back, it seems moving into town was when the fun stopped for us kids. We no longer had the desert to play in, or cows and a garden to provide food. We became more aware too of how poor we were. In the desert the people we knew were much the same as us. Here we could see that other kids were better dressed than us. We still made good friends. It put a big load on us though, because we couldn't keep up with what they had. Sometimes we couldn't even afford shoes.

Under the circumstances, perhaps it's not surprising that Martin was sometimes tempted to just take what he wanted. He could be a thieving little devil for little things. Perhaps it was the thrill of doing it that motivated him, more so than what he took. If he was caught, he treated it as a joke — just as he had done a couple of years earlier in the grocery store in Peoria, when the owner picked him up and shook the candy he had stolen out of his pockets.

When we were living in Glendale, he came running home one time with some watermelons he had stolen. Harley and Charley were with him, but Martin was older and had to be the instigator. It wasn't long before a cop was at the door, and made the boys give back what they had stolen. That time even the cop laughed about it. Even when Martin had done something wrong he managed to get people on his side.

After the divorce, Red returned to Glendale for a while. No one said where he had been. He worked at various odd jobs.

In Glendale there was always a lot of young guys working on cars, motorcycles, or just about anything else. There weren't many jobs at that time, so they had time to think up mischief.

Red and Johnny were very close, and would do things together. One time they made a very crude apparatus to tattoo themselves and the other guys.

Red wanted a sailing ship on his chest. The process was very painful. But he lay there acting like it wasn't hurting, and no doubt the person doing the tattoo was getting a perverse pleasure out of his misery.

Halfway through the procedure, he said he had to have a smoke. He never came back to get the tattoo finished, and he was left with half a sailing ship on his chest. No doubt it became a good conversation piece. He lost a bit of his tough image with the other guys though.

Red was big and tried to give the appearance of being tough. No one ever challenged him that I know of. But, as I have said, he and I were never close. Like my father, Red more or less ignored me. He did hit me once, although not very hard. I screamed anyway, just to see if he would get into trouble. That was when Martin threw a horseshoe at him, hitting him over the eye and leaving a scar. This was long before the fight between Dad and Red. Eventually Red joined the Army and I lost touch with him for a long time.

After being in the service, he moved to California and became a carpenter. He would come back to Glendale once in a while and always seemed happy with his life. Money never seemed to be a problem for him. He spent freely while he was with the family. Personally, I don't think Red was ever mean. He was very proud, and perhaps when I was young I was a little too sensitive about this and took it the wrong way.

Moving into Glendale seemed to have very little effect on Martin.[2] At any rate, he continued to make mischief. No one was safe from his tricks.

One time he broke Harley's little dump truck. He was afraid to tell anyone, so he buried it. Months later he said to Harley: "Promise you won't cry if I tell you where your dump truck is."

Harley promised he wouldn't, and Martin took him to where the truck was buried. Harley set up a howl that could be heard from there to Glendale. I imagine that Martin wanted to put a sock in his mouth right then. But it was too late for him, and he got into a little trouble for making the baby cry. He did seem to enjoy others' discomfort though.

One Fourth of July we were lighting and throwing small firecrackers called Lady Fingers. I threw one that didn't go off. When I picked it up, it went off in my face. It was a very dangerous type of firecracker and has since been banned. Anyway, it stunned me and I didn't know what had happened. I was numb for a while, but when the feeling came back I could feel that my face was swelling. My mouth and nose were puffed up. I was a mess. I must have looked as funny as Harley did when he was stung on the tongue by the ant.

I couldn't cry very well, but I sure wanted to. Typically, Martin took full advantage of my injury to play various practical jokes, such as running away with my things knowing that I was in no condition to chase after him. He laughed for years about the scar on my nose from the firecracker.

Woe betide anyone else who gave me grief though. He was always protective of me, sometimes over protective.

Even though he was too small to excel at high school sports, Martin was friends with guys in the baseball team. They'd hang out together on street corners whistling at girls. Unless I walked by, that is, and then no one dared to. Once there was a new boy with them who didn't know me and made the mistake of whistling. Of course Martin chewed him out. "You don't whistle at my sister," he said. I kinda wished he'd mind his own business!

Girls were a lot more restricted and protected back then, I guess. Martin certainly had a lot more freedom to come and go than I did. If I wanted to go out in the evening, Martin had to chaperone me. He watched every move I made.

Sometimes we would go to the Willow Breeze Ballroom, at 27th Avenue and McDowell. The owner was Sheldon Gibbs, whose band performed there. It was a Western band with guitars, fiddles and an upright bass. They'd do the popular songs of the day, including a lot of Bob Wills type music. I can remember Sheldon Gibbs singing "I'm Looking Over A Four-Leaf Clover" as if it were yesterday. Marty would get up and sing with them. This was before he got paid for being on stage.[3]

You'd think he would have lightened up on me by the time we were adults. But no. Soon after I married I went to see him perform at Fred Kare's club in Phoenix with some girlfriends. Marty wouldn't speak to me. He said, "Where's your husband? Get home to him."

Later, he was a bit the same way with his wife Marizona, I noticed. He could be domineering with her. With her long dresses and hair pulled back, I thought she had a Holy Roller look. I wonder now whether part of her attraction for him was that he felt she was somebody he could keep in the background.

In one area, and one area alone, I was able to show Martin what to do. When I was staying with my cousins, I had attended some country dances where my Uncle Mart played the fiddle. Later I taught Martin the steps I'd learned.

From the age of about 14 through high school, I spent the summers staying with our sister Ann at the grocery store she ran in south Phoenix. That's where I taught Martin to dance. We would go into a storage room behind Ann's house and practice in secret.

I remember we played a record of "When The Moon Comes Over The Mountain," the song made famous by radio star of the time, Kate Smith. I don't remember whether she was singing this particular version. To us it seemed a draggy old waltz, but it served the purpose.

Whenever we heard a noise outside one or other of us would whisper, "Stop, stop." Martin in particular didn't want anyone to find out what we were doing. He didn't want anyone to see him make a mistake.

He quickly learned the basic steps, and we got really, really good at dancing together. In fact, for a while he would never dance with anyone else. We made our own steps, and we would win little jitterbug contests at the Willow Breeze. "The Yellow Rose of Texas" was another song I can remember being a favorite with us around that time. And "San Antonio Rose." Boy, Martin and I could really dance to that.

People thought we were dating. We got so good, and I was so proud. It was the only thing I ever taught him how to do. You see, he could do everything. He could skate, he could ride a bicycle first, he could swim. I couldn't swim because he would try to drown me every time I got in the water. The boys would come over and hold me down. When I'd try to skate he'd push me down. So I gave up easily. It was either that or die young. Then gradually he started dancing with other girls, and he was on his way again.

Overall, high school was a trying time for me. Mom never showed love for me the way I wanted. I think I understand it better now than I did then. She'd spent her life raising kids and trying to keep her marriage together, and maybe as a young female I represented something she'd lost along the way.

At times though, I felt I didn't get much credit. When Martin dropped out after about a year and a half of high school, for instance, Mom was really mad because I stayed on to graduate. I had to take a job after school so that I could afford clothes and other things I needed. Mom wanted me to follow my brother's example and quit school and work fulltime. She never did get over it.

Not that Martin was that successful at getting a job. I remember Uncle Mart took him up to the mountains to work, but it didn't last long. Martin didn't like to work.

When he did have paycheck though, he could be generous with it. His first paycheck that I remember was from working in the projection room at the El-Ray theater in Glendale, and he used it to buy a sack of Christmas presents for the family.

I refuse now, and refused then most of the time, to believe that Martin was a bad boy. He was spoiled in the sense that he had no discipline. Mom simply refused to see that he was in the wrong so much of the time. The older boys resented her favoritism and did what they could to make him unhappy. But mostly we all fought a losing battle with him. Fortunately for me, I loved him and knew that he loved me, and so I saw a side of him that was unfamiliar to the younger and older ones.

Notes

[1] As a beginner, Marty faced one of the toughest audiences he would ever have to face. His older brothers made such fun of him when he tried to play guitar that he had to leave the house and find somewhere else to practice, according to his friend of that time, Ralph Ramsey. Apparently Marty walked across the street with his guitar to Ralph's house, where the reception was much warmer.

It was this same friend who later sold Marty what was probably his first car — for $12. It was an Overland, which Marty's older brothers had converted to a pick-up by putting a Model T body on the chassis. Unfortunately they had stripped a thread on the steering column in assembling the vehicle. Marty was driving back from visiting friends in Peoria when he had to brake to avoid another car. The steering column came off in his hands, and Marty ended up in a roadside trench with an overturned car. Not for the last time, he was able to walk away from a wreck without serious injury.

Ralph also said that the older brothers and he used the Overland to make night raids on neighboring farmland. They'd take vegetables from the fields for Mrs. Robinson to cook — what they told her about the origin of the vegetables he didn't say — and they'd steal gasoline from storage tanks used to refuel tractors. Once the brothers were caught and spent time in jail, but Ralph and Marty were not involved in that escapade.

[2] It did have an effect on his music though. Marty recalled sitting on the back porch in the evening — "We lived in the last house on the white side before you got to the railroad tracks" — and listening to singers and guitarists in Glendale's Mexican Town on the other side of the tracks. *The Nashville Tennessean*, October 10th, 1971.

In time, those influences no doubt would filter into those exhilarating south-of-the-border arrangements for his gunfighter ballads and trail songs.

[3] The Gibbs band featured members of the Herndon family, which in recent years has had a prominent part in the Phoenix area music scene as owners and resident band at Scottsdale's Handlebar J nightclub.

A generation after the Gibbs Band was in its prime, singer/guitarist Ray Herndon gained national recognition in Lyle Lovett's backing band and then moved to Nashville to make a name in his own right.

Incidentally, although written in 1927, "I'm Looking Over A Four-Leaf Clover" didn't circulate widely until Art Mooney's recording in

1948. So was the Gibbs band ahead of Mooney, or was Mamie remembering things out of sequence?

Chapter Twelve
Reflections from Marty's Naval Service and Early Singing Career

Childhood with Marty, when the twins were almost inseparable, was the most vivid period in Mamie's memory.

She had less to say about his late teenage years, and contact between them became even more erratic as they reached adulthood. Mamie married, and even when there was the opportunity for them to get together, she remembered, Marty insisted that her husband should be present at their meetings. It was a protocol, one would imagine, that might put a strain on intimate discussion between the siblings.

With World War Two, Marty went into uniform like millions of others. In his case, he enlisted in the Navy at the age of 17 in 1943 and spent three years serving on an LCM (landing craft mechanized) in the Pacific.[1]

In addition to their crews of four or five — deckhands, a machinist or engineer and a coxswain — these vessels of approximately 50 feet in length were designed to carry about 150 men or a medium sized tank. Upon reaching land, a ramp at the bow end could be lowered to allow the men or equipment aboard to disembark. LCMs were also used as floating platforms from which to fire 4.2-inch mortars at targets on land.[2]

Size apparently determined Martin's duties. Recruits were divided by height. Tall men were picked to be coxswains; they had to be tall to be able to see all around them as they steered the landing craft. Shorter guys, like Martin, manned 50 caliber machine guns, operated the ramp and other general duties. Nonetheless, deckhands were expected to be versatile in such skills as seamanship, boat handling, some engineering, knowledge of signaling and communications, gunnery, navigation, and weather lore. They were expected to be capable of stepping in if more senior crew members were injured.

Most likely Marty trained in San Diego before shipping out to the Solomon Islands, to the east of Australia and Papua New Guinea.

A local newspaper report of the time in the *Glendale Herald* stated that Seaman 1st class Martin Robinson landed on the island of Bougainville in November 1943 with the first U.S. forces to invade. His much older half-brother Pat was reported to have been in the war's other great theater of seaborne invasion, in France, while brother George (Red) served with a searchlight division stationed in Long Beach, California.

It's likely Martin's landing craft was involved in establishing beachheads with the Marines in the campaign of 1943 to oust the Japanese from the island of Bougainville. He must have arrived too late to perform similar duties during the better known battle for Guadalcanal, which took place the previous year.

When they weren't active in the fighting, the sailors apparently lived in tents on one or other of the islands. There were four men to a tent, and in the center of each was a foxhole covered with logs. They were commonly known as bunkers. Whatever the description, they were sorely needed. Although the Japanese were being forced back, they continued to bomb, and warning sirens were a nightly occurrence in this tent city.

Even under these circumstances, Marty showed his natural inclination to entertain. Apparently he was able to lay his hands on a guitar, although whether he won any fans at this point in his musical career is open to speculation. Later he told acquaintances he began playing while he was in the Navy to counter boredom. That must have been between the excitement of the bombing raids.

He also got some attention as a boxer, staging sparring matches with a lofty Native American known, predictably, as Big Chief. The spectacle of this large man climbing in the ring with the feisty little Martin Robinson must have been enough in itself to pull a crowd. The sparring was good natured enough and it must have made quite a show in a place where opportunities for a sports spectacle were pretty limited presumably. As Mamie remarked when she heard about it during our research, "That would be what Martin wanted — to get an audience."

Contact with home during his time in the Pacific was sporadic, of course. One communication that did reach the front was the weekly hometown newspaper. In fact, Martin wrote to the *Glendale Herald* to express his appreciation. The first thought after daily work is usually of home, he wrote, and after receiving a copy of the *Herald* he read it three times "and found something new each time." Keep it coming, he continued, "and help us win our fight against homesickness."

There were also spells of leave. During one of them, Mamie and Martin had to celebrate their birthday a day early. This they did with a dinner at their mother's home at 47 South Fourth Avenue in Glendale. On their birthday itself, Martin was due to return to duty.

Mamie had also visited her brother in San Diego after he completed boot camp. A surviving photo shows the two siblings visiting the city's famous zoo.

Whether it was because of a reluctance to talk about the war or a lack of opportunity for Mamie to bring up the subject, Martin kept this period pretty much a closed chapter as far as his twin sister was concerned.

"I don't remember him talking about the Navy that much," she confessed when it came time to write down her recollections.

*** *** ***

After returning to Glendale in 1946, Martin didn't settle easily into civilian life. He tried a few jobs without showing a preference for any particular line of work. When he eventually started to make headway as an entertainer, he told at least one acquaintance that he initially pursued music as a preferred alternative to holding down a day job.

One man who played a role in Marty's musical development at this point was fellow Arizona singer Frankie Starr, whose claim it was to have given Marty "his first job in music."[3]

Eleven years Marty's senior, Starr was performing in local night clubs with his band when Marty came back from the Navy. Marty apparently tracked down Frankie at a local club after hearing him sing on his radio show on Phoenix's KPHO.

Like others who knew Marty in his early years, Starr's first impression from this 1947 meeting was that he was "dirt poor."

"He was real thin, a real skinny little boy," Starr remembered, "and his thinness made him look like he had a nose like Jimmy Durante. He had a big wide nose, and his face was so thin it kinda amplified his nose."

Marty's staple outfit was "an old pair of Levis, with the pocket out and his wallet about to drop out the back. He had a little white tee shirt and a pair of loafers, that you used to put dimes in. That was it. That's all I ever saw him in."

Perhaps his limited wardrobe as a kid explains why Marty later wrote one of his biggest hits, "A White Sport Coat (And A Pink Carnation)," to say nothing of his liking for the colorful, rhinestone-studded Nudie suits he customarily wore on stage as a star.

Marty told Frankie he was driving a truck but wanted to quit that to get into the music business.

"He was making very little money, driving a truck working 10 or 11 hours a day hauling brick. He worked all hours. Jobs weren't too easy to get back then."

Starr invited him on stage — he was performing at a club called Vern and Don's on the main drag into Phoenix, East Van Buren Street, at the time — and Marty sang an Eddy Arnold song, "Many Tears Ago." It must have been enough to convince Frankie that the young man had promise because he bought Marty clothes and musical equipment.

They went to Porter's clothing store, where Marty got kitted out with "a nice Western pinstriped suit and coat, shirt, tie, boots."

The suit was "a kinda coal charcoal…And then I bought him a pair of Western pants and a matching shirt."

From what Starr said, Marty was even worse off in terms of his musical equipment.

"He had an old guitar with a bent neck. There was a piece of car inner tube wrapped around it to hold the pickup on to the box. It was an acoustic guitar with a homemade pickup."

Once again Starr helped out, buying Marty a guitar and amplifier at a local Mecca for instruments, Otto Stein Music Company, in downtown Phoenix. The guitar was "a little Epiphone that had a hollow body but it was strictly electric," Starr said.

The next step was to get Marty membership in the appropriate union, the American Federation of Musicians, and then at least he had the basic requirements he would need to face an audience.

There would even be an early attempt to give Marty a stage name, with Starr suggesting Marty Martin. That name, of course, failed to stick. In turn, Marty called his mentor "Pops" — a substitute perhaps for the father with whom he had broken off contact by this time.

As a novice, Marty was a shadow of the man who later won a reputation for being reluctant to end performances. He still suffered from the shyness Mamie had observed when he sang in church as a child.

Compared to the voice familiar from recordings, Starr said, Marty "sang altogether different" when he started out as a stage performer. His guitar style too left room for improvement, consisting as it did of a few basic strummed chords. As a little boy, Starr continued, Marty had guitar lessons from a friend of his, Charles 'Monk' Ray. But it seems these didn't go beyond the rudiments.[4]

Before Starr admitted Marty to his band he got him a solo gig at another Van Buren nightspot, the Gallup Inn. On the night of Marty's first performance the plan was for them to meet later, after they had both finished their gigs, and then they'd get a sandwich. But apparently nerves cut Marty's solo spot short. Starr had only been performing for about 20 minutes when Marty came into Vern and Don's.

"He had his guitar under one arm and this little amplifier," Starr recollected, "and he walked in somewhat dejected and walks straight across the dance floor and he said, 'Pops, they don't want to hear me sing.' So I said, 'Well, if you can hang in there, Marty, with your job, when we get more business I'll hire you.'"

Eventually that's what happened, and Marty went from about $27 a week driving a truck to a union rate of $60 plus about $30 in tips.

"His eyes lit up," Starr said. "He couldn't believe it."

Even with the reassurance of being on stage with Starr and his band, Marty still lacked self-confidence.

"He couldn't look at people," Starr added. "He'd sing with his head down. I'd say, 'Tell 'em we're gonna take an intermission.' He'd say, 'You tell 'em, you tell 'em.'"

According to Starr, one of the club owners got frustrated with Marty's early efforts. Frankie had to step in and defend his sideman.

"(Marty) only knew eight or 10 songs. He kept singing them over and over again. Vern came to me and said, 'You're gonna have to let that guy go. He's driving me crazy singing those songs over and over again.'"

Supposedly Marty was also getting into trouble with some of the club patrons.

"He was always worried about someone shooting him," Starr said, "because he'd make a pass at every woman who came in."[5]

Starr said he refused to fire Marty. In time there must have been a noticeable improvement in his protégé because, when Starr decided to move on from the club, Marty took over as featured performer.

Eventually the club was sold to a Chicagoan, Fred Kare. One anecdote from this period that did reach Mamie was about a nightly ritual that took place during Marty's gigs at the club. His audience used to shout out, "Who cares?" and Marty replied, "I don't know. Who cares?" and they would say, "Fred Kare's."

By the time he was ready to move on to bigger things, Marty had won quite a following it seems. A couple of interviews with people who knew him then mention that the club owner — presumably Fred Kare — bought a bus ticket to Nashville for Marty when he was invited to perform at the Grand Ole Opry for the first time. Apparently he'd come a long way from driving club owners so crazy they wanted him fired.

Notes

[1] Much of the information about Martin's naval service came from an interview Mamie and I conducted with one Frank DeBeery or DeBerry, who at that time was living in Yuma, Arizona, and had met Martin in the service. They didn't train together, but Mr. DeBerry/DeBeery did serve with him on landing crafts in the Solomon Islands and they bumped into each other on at least one occasion back in Phoenix after the war.

How Mamie and Mr. DeBerry/DeBeery were put in contact with each other I can no longer recall, if I ever knew. Unfortunately, my efforts to trace Mr. DeBerry/DeBeery's family were not successful.

[2] Different sources vary on the details. I used two main sources for the technical information: 1) *Gunboats, Amphibious Employment of the 4.2-inch Mortar*, compiled & edited by Jack Butler, veteran of the 82nd Chemical Mortar Battalion, who in turn credits.a history of the Chemical Warfare Service (CWS) published by the Army's Office of Military History and 2) *Skill in the Surf, A Landing Boat Manual* published by the military in 1945.

[3] It's hard to gauge the late Frankie Starr's relationship with Marty, because by the time I interviewed him his memories were clouded by the conviction that his own singing career had been derailed by Marty.

According to Starr, when Marty moved to Music City he wrote back that he'd make contacts for his friend but not to relocate yet because it was so hard for a newcomer to get noticed. Frankie and his wife June got impatient and moved to Nashville all the same, "and we damn near starved to death."

Starr was encouraged though by headway he was making with a single he'd written and recorded with Decca Records, "That's The Way The Big Ball Bounces" paired with "I Don't Care What You Used To Be."

At that point in his career a dispute resurfaced about some songs Marty had written before leaving Glendale and supposedly given to Starr to be published in a songbook, with any profits to be shared between the two of them.

Rumors circulated that Starr had stolen 13 songs from Marty for this project. Starr conjectured that Marty was becoming insecure about his one-time boss's rising fortunes and used this issue to kill his career.

In any event, Starr felt he was ostracized in Nashville from then on, and as a result returned to Phoenix — and relative obscurity.

In June 1984, at the time of this interview, Starr was still brandishing the notarized form on which Marty had signed over his rights to these 13 songs. Starr said he had many offers over the years to record or sell the songs, and in fact in 1983 Starr was so impressed with a young singer named Ron Hall that he allowed him to record two of the songs Marty had signed over.

The resulting single, featuring the Robbins compositions "Our Love Is At An End" and "For A Lifetime," was recorded at Chaton Recordings studio in Scottsdale, Arizona, and released on Starr's own Star-Win label. Curiously, where one would look for the songwriting credit on the record there is only Frankie's name. No mention of Marty at all.

Of course, Marty was not around by that time to give his own version of these events, even if he had been so inclined. In answer to Starr's requests, he did write a rather noncommittal letter in 1976 acknowledging the notarized statement but skirting around the question of the rumors about which Starr had complained.

Mamie, for her part, probably would have conceded Frankie Starr's need to tell his side of the story. The two had discussed the saga of the 13 songs and, by Frankie's reckoning, Mamie felt he'd earned some right to them — for one thing, by virtue of the mental anguish he'd gone through over it.

[4] Mamie said she had no recollection of lessons and that Marty never mentioned any. Her version was that Marty more or less taught himself from picking up his sister Ann's guitar when they were about 11. She remembered Monk Ray though. In her eyes as a child, he was "a funny looking old man who played the fiddle."

[5] I include some of these details to try to give a fuller portrait of how Marty was seen by someone who worked with him on a nightly basis. At

the same time, I'm sure others had a different view of him, and of course once again it would be fairer if Marty could give his own account of this period.

Chapter Thirteen
Buenos Dias Arizona

Even though Mamie had moved to Parker with her husband, the twins shared some memorable occasions. Chief among these was Marty and Marizona's wedding on September 27th, 1948.

Marty sprung a surprise on his sister by announcing he wanted to get married in the church in Parker on their birthday. Mamie had only met the bride once before, when she had come out to Parker for a brief visit.

The plan didn't work out quite the way Marty wanted because he had to work on their birthday. The couple arrived the following day though, apparently having picked up the marriage license in the town of Salome on the way.

The ceremony was conducted by the Reverend Gertrude Parker. What she thought of the groom making faces at Mamie during the service can only be guessed at. As usual Marty had to ham it up, and his sister couldn't resist being a receptive audience. Marizona, so sweet and religious in Mamie's eyes, was more in keeping with the solemnity of the event.

Typically hard up, Marty only had a ten and a five dollar bill on him. He intended to slip the five to the preacher in payment, but the two bills stuck together and the Rev. Parker got both. He was sick about it, his sister recalled. Anyway, it didn't stop the happy couple from honeymooning across the river in a cabin in Earp, the town so named because famed 1880s lawman Wyatt Earp had lived there.

Even though Marty must have started getting some attention locally as a performer, he was still living hand to mouth. On at least one occasion he hopped a freight train to visit Mamie in Parker.

"He wouldn't work," Mamie recounted. "All he wanted to do was music, and at that time nobody ever thought he would be a star. I don't even think he thought he would be a star."

Mamie and her husband contributed a little financial aid to the newly weds. Even so, daily life must have been pretty lean for them. Mamie visited them once in the trailer where they lived behind Marty's mom's house in Glendale. All they'd had to eat for days, Mamie said, was cream of wheat.

"I felt so sad," she remembered, "but I thought he'd never do any better."

It actually got worse. At a nightclub in Yuma where he was performing, Marty was accused of stealing beer. Unlike the hero of his big hit "El Paso," Marty wasn't able to make a quick getaway and so he ended up in jail for the night. Someone else had been the thief, Marty claimed, and apparently he was believed. All the same, Mamie said, that overnight detention taught her brother a lesson he never wanted to repeat.

By the time Marty and Marizona moved to Nashville in 1953, Mamie was a mother with the first of two sons, Danny, and "was in her own little world." But there was still contact between brother and sister. In July, for instance, they had their annual exchange of Christmas presents. Why July? For an upcoming country star, time for family get togethers must have been at a premium around the end of the year.

Mamie never ceased to look up to her brother. "I was in awe of him all my life," she said. In times of stress, such as when her son Daniel died in a construction accident, Marty was always ready to give his support — by phone if his schedule didn't allow him to be there in person. And he continued to be the brother who could do anything he set his mind to, with the exception of being a good student in earlier years of course. On a visit to Parker, for example, Marty tried water skiing for the first time. Before the session was through, he was riding along on one ski.

Considering how much larger than life Marty seemed as an entertainer, it's strange to think that Mamie's lasting impression was that her brother became a loner in later life. After performances in Las Vegas, she remembered, his entourage would go off to enjoy the nightlife. Not Marty though. He went right to his room, with Mamie in tow if she was around. As in their youth, the protective brother emerged — and he wasn't about to let his twin sister go off unchaperoned.

*** *** ***

Marty, of course, would go from success to success from this point on. He gravitated from being a club resident to having his own show on KTYL radio in Mesa, Arizona, and then moving to KPHO AM-TV in Phoenix to headline a half-hour show called "Chuck Wagon Time," with his newly assembled band, the K-Bar Cowboys. Subsequently he transferred to television, although legend has it that Marty at first refused to go in front of the cameras, explaining that he was scared to do a live TV show.[1]

He was persuaded to do the show all the same, and word of his talent spread as far as Nashville. This was aided by an influential ally, KPHO's general manager Harry Stone, a former Nashville big wheel who evidently recognized latent talent when he heard it and was instrumental in lining up a recording contract in May 1951 with Columbia Records.[2]

And so in 1952 Marty moved to country music's capital with his wife, the former Marizona Baldwin, whom he had met while she was working in Upton's Ice Cream Parlor at the corner of 58th and Glendale Avenue.[3]

His career as an international star has been well documented. He was one of the first to have hits on both the country and pop charts, writing an estimated 500 songs and topping the country music charts 18 times. From 1953 onwards, he was a much-anticipated regular at country music's Mecca, the Grand Ole Opry.

His first country top 10 listing came the year after he moved to Nashville, with his own composition, "I'll Go On Alone." Three and a half years later, he finally reached the top of the charts with the pop-oriented "Singing The Blues," giving him the crossover hit that made him an undisputed star.[4]

Probably for diehard fans though his more lasting legacy stemmed from the Western material he wrote. His Grammy-winning hit "El Paso," recounting the story of a love-blinded cowboy, is the best known of a catalog of narrative ballads and reflective songs about the characters, gunfights and places of days gone by. So many of his songs, with their Mexican-flavored guitar and trumpet arrangements, are saturated in Arizonan atmosphere.

Marty was clearly haunted by this history. In the lyrics of "El Paso City," written 17 years after his greatest hit, he even mused about whether he had lived a previous life in those turbulent times. Like so many of the characters in his songs, he seemed to yearn for the open space of the frontier. "I cannot stand two weeks in one place," he once said in regard to his performing schedule.[5]

In the same way as he strove to span musical styles and settings, he was ambitious to add to his resume as an entertainer in general.

Movie roles attracted him in particular — not surprising after his boyhood infatuation with Gene Autry. He starred in *Guns Of A Stranger*, a movie designed to revive the singing cowboy genre. It was filmed at Apache Land, the now-burned movie town in what became Gold Canyon, 40 miles east of Phoenix, and included bit parts for his kid brothers Harley and Charley. His last movie role was a cameo part in Clint Eastwood's *Honkytonk Man* in 1982. Marty turned his hand to prose as well, with a short Western novel entitled *The Small Man*.[6]

Above all, he left a lasting impression as a stock car driver. He excelled in the sport, and among his peers he was rated as professional quality. If the singing hadn't worked out, an alternative career might have led in the direction of NASCAR. He competed in top events, such as the Daytona 500, and in 1972 survived a 150 mph crash.

Even as a patient he blazed trails. At Nashville's St. Thomas Hospital, where he died, he had been one of the first patients to undergo coronary bypass surgery 12 years previously.

After a second heart attack, in 1980, Marty reflected that he "had experienced death so many times I should be dead. I don't know why God has let me go on living, but I'm glad he did."

Understandably, Marty continued to have a close attachment to the hospital, and his portrait was on the cover of the hospital's 1982 financial report.[7]

For Mamie, her brother's life in the fast lane must have been a frequent source of anxiety. Even as a girl she'd "always been afraid of something," in contrast with her try-anything-for-a-laugh brother.

After his career took off, he traveled so much that she wouldn't look at the papers in case there was news of Martin being in a plane crash or some such disaster. As for his racing, she "kinda blocked it out." But she had faith in him too. When he told her, after his first heart operation, that he could "do anything I did before, only better," she took him at his word. She never considered he would have more heart trouble, and the shock of his death was all the greater for it.

Marty's impact continued to resonate after his death. Within months, readers of the influential *Music City News* chose his album *Come Back To Me* and single "Some Memories Just Won't Die" as their top choices for the year. Two months before his death, incidentally, he had been inducted into the Country Music Hall of Fame.

It is ironic, considering how much he loved Arizona and the Western heritage, that there are more tangible tributes to Marty outside the state than within it.

He spent his career based in the Nashville area, of course, and his grave in the city's Woodlawn Cemetery has become an obvious shrine for his fans. In addition, the west Texas town of El Paso has recognized him with a plaque in the city's airport and by naming a park after him.

Back in Arizona, Glendale does have a Marty Robbins Plaza in an alley behind what used to be Upton's Ice Cream Parlor, but attempts over the years to give him a more prominent memorial where he grew up have so far come to nothing.

Such statistics and observations are largely beyond the scope of this book, in any case.

The aim here has been to forego the career perspective and concentrate instead on Mamie's memories of him and the years when he was still an Arizona boy. Throughout this account, I have tried to remain true to Mamie's viewpoint.

Mamie remained immensely proud of her brother's achievements. Despite their diverging paths in life, I think she always felt there was that special psychic bond between them, the kind that seems to connect twins even when distance and time come between them.

Notes

[1] This is how it was told in *Marty Robbins*, a souvenir booklet from the Marty Robbins museum that existed in the '80s in Hendersonville, near Nashville. He got over his fear of the small screen, of course, and made numerous TV appearances, including the Western-oriented series "The Drifter," made when television was still in black and white.

[2] The same booklet credits Nashville star Little Jimmy Dickens, a guest on Marty's TV show, with securing the Columbia Records deal and Stone for getting him on the Grand Ole Opry for the first time.

This account goes on to say Fred Rose, of the noted music publishing company Acuff-Rose, flew to Phoenix to sign Marty as a songwriter. "This is the highest compliment I have ever been paid," Marty is quoted as saying.

Mamie, incidentally, said she had always heard that Harry Stone made the Columbia connection.

[3] Mamie and Marizona apparently didn't get along well — according to the former anyway, and since Marizona is no longer with us her side of the story will remain undisclosed presumably.

Mamie insisted that Marty's composition "My Woman, My Woman, My Wife," which won him a second Grammy in 1970, was written originally with his mother in mind.

On July 10th, 2001, Marizona died of cancer in Phoenix. Seeking treatment, she had returned to her childhood haunts from Franklin,

Tennessee, where she had lived with Marty for so much of their married life.

[4] The song saturated pop consciousness at the time, with other high profile versions from Guy Mitchell and Britain's Tommy Steele.

[5] *The Arizona Republic*, June 18th, 1980.

[6] At least one name in Marty's story had a basis in real life. Tolf Lacy, introduced as a boy in the story, was also the name of an old deaf man who lived near the twins when they were about eight, Mamie said. One day their mother sent them over to see if Mr. Lacy had a couple of envelopes she could have. The children delivered their request as loudly as they felt was appropriate, but the old man didn't grasp it. "Cantelopes?" he asked. "I don't have any cantelopes." Apparently the two kids got a laugh out of this for a long time. Tolf in the story also gets into trouble with his slingshot — another detail that had a parallel in Marty's own activities.

[7] The information about Marty's relationship with St. Thomas Hospital came from the *Phoenix Gazette*, December 9th, 1982.

*** *** ***

Printed in the United States
75992LV00002B/280-348

9 781601 451057